Closing the Circle

Closing the Circle

A Practical Guide to Implementing Literacy Reform, K-12

Sean A. Walmsley

JOSSEY-BASS
A Wiley Imprint
www.josseybass.com

Published by Jossey-Bass
A Wiley Imprint
989 Market Street, San Francisco, CA 94103-1741—www.josseybass.com

Library of Congress Cataloging-in-Publication Data

Walmsley, Sean A.
    Closing the circle: a practical guide to implementing literacy reform, K-12 / Sean Walmsley.—1st ed.
      p.   cm.—(The Jossey-Bass education series)
    Includes bibliographical references and index.
    ISBN 978-0-7879-9637-6 (cloth)
      1. Language arts—United States.   2. Educational change—United States.
    3. Literacy—United States.   I. Title.
    LB1576.W259   2008
    428.0071—dc22

                                         2007049556

Printed in the United States of America
FIRST EDITION
HB Printing   10 9 8 7 6 5 4 3 2 1

2/18/09

The Jossey-Bass Education Series

Exhibits

*For Katharine and Jen . . . and in fond
memory of Peter Mosenthal*

Contents

Preface

This book is about reshaping language arts in America's elementary, middle, and secondary schools. It presents a simple, coherent framework for aligning literacy expectations, instruction, instructional support, and assessment, and reporting and analyzing data.

Who Should Be Reading This Book?

The book is deliberately titled *Closing the Circle: A Practical Guide to Implementing Literacy Reform, K–12* because it seamlessly connects each of the components of the framework and offers practical advice on how to make this happen. Although the book is grounded in current literacy theory and pedagogy, its primary goal is to help practitioners—district and school administrators, curriculum supervisors, literacy coaches, classroom teachers, reading and literacy specialists, and special educators—work together in more thoughtful and productive ways to achieve better literacy outcomes for students, K–12. Because the book grew out of a graduate course taught by the author and was put into practice in public schools over several decades, it clearly is intended as a text or supplementary reading in both administrative and literacy-related course work, especially at the graduate level. But it might also be welcomed by parents who want to understand the full breadth of K–12 language arts and the role they might best play in their children's literacy development across these thirteen years.

District and School Administrators

Superintendents, assistant superintendents for curriculum, language arts coordinators, and school principals will find the book useful as they ponder what they can do to focus on what really matters in language arts, K–12, and to better coordinate their language arts programs across the board. The framework's broad perspective gives administrators the "big picture" of what counts as being literate, as well as a K–12 panorama, so that they can think more clearly about what's important to include in overall language arts goals and how these goals can be implemented across thirteen or more years of a student's elementary, middle, and high school education. But the book also shows how to bring the various elements of a language arts program under control, so that expectations, curriculum, and assessment, as well as reporting and analyzing data, are tightly woven together from an administrative point of view.

Curriculum and Language Arts Administrators

Curriculum supervisors, language arts coordinators, and literacy coaches have significant responsibilities for the content of language arts programs across the grades. The book addresses these issues in great detail, because in recent years, language arts teaching has suffered from imbalances between different components of language arts, resulting in uneven and often haphazard coverage of important literacy skills and insufficient literacy experiences (for example, students not having read or written enough on their own). Getting the balance right and figuring out how to fit it all in, both within and across the grades, is a serious challenge, and the history of literacy instruction over the past fifteen years is one of pendulum-swinging and imbalances. Even balanced literacy isn't really balanced.

Classroom Teachers

Classroom teachers should benefit from the big-picture perspective of the framework, but they will surely appreciate the simplicity and clarity of the literacy expectations (a far cry from the 250–300 skills per grade level), as well as the notion of the few must-do instructional activities necessary in every classroom, to contribute to the literacy expectations. But they will also applaud the importance of building on teacher strengths and the need for differentiated instruction to meet the needs of increasingly diverse students. The framework offers classroom teachers practical ways to teach what matters in language arts by doing less but doing it better—and doing it as part of a K–12 team rather than in isolation.

Literacy Specialists, Special Educators

Although literacy specialists and special educators should learn a great deal from the overall framework, there is a chapter devoted to instructional support, and it shows how the new federal Response to Intervention (RTI) initiative (Individuals with Disabilities Education Act, 2004 authorization) both complements and supports the framework. This legislation challenges not only the traditional definition of literacy disabilities; it also promotes entirely different instructional, assessment, and organizational strategies for addressing the needs of struggling students. Under this legislation, classroom teachers, as well as instructional support specialists, have to work together in much more efficient and coordinated ways, so this book will be useful for all educators who teach struggling learners.

College Faculty

If the book's primary audience is practitioners in the field, then those who prepare practitioners should also find it useful in courses and workshops for administrators, teachers, and specialists. As accountability for student outcomes increases and is equally shared among administrators and teachers, colleges need to prepare administrators, classroom teachers, and specialists for these new roles. Administrators need to have greater knowledge of literacy content, as well as ways to organize and coordinate K–12 programs. Teachers and specialists need to have both a broad perspective on K–12 literacy and know how best to contribute to each student's literacy progress toward well-defined expectations. There needs to be room in the graduate courses these educators take for both of these perspectives, and this book makes its contribution to both aspects.

Staff Developers

Since this book is subtitled *A Practical Guide to Implementing Literacy Reform, K–12*, it is especially useful for staff developers or consultants who organize or provide professional development in literacy. Staff developers will probably find the simplicity and clarity of literacy attributes compelling, and they will appreciate the practical suggestions for implementing the various components, as well as how to relate attributes, curriculum, instructional support, assessment, and reporting.

Parents

Finally, this book has much to offer parents as they think about their own children's K–12 language arts experiences. The parents are the only people, other than the children themselves, who understand the experience of moving from grade to grade. This book gives parents not only a bird's-eye view of the entire K–12 language arts continuum, but it also provides them with a way to examine the language arts instruction and experiences their children are receiving. It shows parents examples of report cards that give them really useful information about strengths and needs of their children across all language arts, and there's a sample parent guide that suggests useful contributions they can make to their children's literacy progress.

What's in the Book?

The Preamble answers the question, Why a new language arts framework? by pointing out limitations in traditional ways of articulating and organizing language arts across the grades and suggesting that a fresh approach is needed.

Chapter One—"A Simple Framework for Language Arts"—articulates the basic theoretical foundations for a new framework. It then goes on to briefly describe the major components of the approach—articulating literacy expectations (which are here called attributes), teaching and organizing language arts, providing instructional support, conducting assessment, reporting student progress, and analyzing data to inform instruction. This chapter gives an overview of the whole framework, followed by chapters that describe each of the components in much finer detail.

Chapter Two—"Literacy Attributes"—defines literacy attributes (our expectations for what we want a student to know, do, understand, and have experienced in language arts, K–12). It explains similarities and differences between literacy attributes, skills, and standards, and provides examples to illustrate them.

Chapter Three—"Teaching Language Arts"—presents a new approach for teaching the K–12 language arts curriculum—the concept of *instructional contributions* (what teachers do to help children learn). These contributions include "non-negotiable" (that is, *all* teachers must supply them) instruction and experiences, with a range of instructional activities that implement the non-negotiables. Examples of non-negotiables and the instructional activities that implement them are provided.

Chapter Four—"Organizing Language Arts Instruction"—focuses on the "containers," or structures, within which language arts activities are organized and scheduled. These include commercial basal reading series, theme-based, literature-based, genres, workshops, and literacy across the curriculum.

Chapter Five—"Instructional Support"—makes the case for integrating instructional support into the framework, shows how the new federal initiative RTI complements the framework, and again provides examples to illustrate best practices.

Chapter Six—"Assessment"—lays out principles for assessment within an attributes approach and describes techniques for gathering evidence on students' current status and progress toward acquiring each of the literacy attributes. This chapter also addresses the design and content of report cards.

Chapter Seven—"Reporting"—makes the case for keeping parents informed, so they know their child's status and progress toward each of the literacy attributes. In most school districts, report cards are not well aligned with literacy expectations and the curriculum. This chapter also describes ways to keep the community informed about the district's progress toward its literacy goals.

Chapter Eight—"Analyzing Data to Inform Instruction"— describes ways that districts can analyze assessment data from a variety of sources to inform literacy instruction. Although assessment includes the same data as are shared on report cards, it also uses raw data that teachers and specialists routinely gather in their classrooms but don't consider appropriate to place on report cards.

Chapter Nine—"Implementing the Framework"—is written as a guide for school districts interested in implementing all or parts of the language arts framework. It describes a number of different ways the author has worked with schools and provides insights based on experiences working in a variety of school settings.

Finally, Chapter Ten—"Reflections on the Promise and Challenge of Effective Language Arts Reform"—considers reform principles that seem to work well (for example, keeping it simple but not simplistic; valuing opposing points of view) and some that continue to challenge all who would undertake serious literacy reforms (for example, how to sustain them and how to spread literacy across the entire curriculum).

Acknowledgments

It is hard to know where to begin in acknowledging the debt I owe to so many colleagues, graduate students, educators, and friends with whom I have shared the journey that has culminated in the publication of this book.

I'll start by thanking my present and former colleagues in the Reading Department at SUNY-Albany—for their diverse perspectives on literacy, and their commitment to advancing literacy theory and solving real-world literacy issues, especially with underserved student populations. I'm lucky to have Peter Johnston, Rose Weber, Jim Collins, Ginny Goatley, George Kamberelis, Donna Scanlon, Cheryl Dozier, Margi Sheehy, and Kelly Wissman as colleagues; and Dick Allington and Jim Fleming as former colleagues. I am particularly grateful to Ginny Goatley for stepping in as chair so I could take a sabbatical leave to complete this work, and to Dean Susan Phillips for her support. I am also hugely appreciative of the contributions made by graduate students in my course, Administering and Reforming School Literacy Programs. Several chapters were written and rewritten in response to their questions and concerns.

Administrators, teachers, students, and parents in the many schools I've worked with over the years have shaped and refined my thinking, and without their support and trust, this book might simply have been a collection of lectures from a graduate course. Among the many districts I have worked with, several stand out: Manchester Center in Vermont, and Cairo-Durham, Gilbertsville-Mt. Upton, Carmel, Putnam Valley, Hunter-Tannersville, Brewster, Harrison, and Ossining—all in New York.

While he was principal in Manchester Center Elementary School, Dick Leadem challenged me to articulate literacy attributes and set me on the path that leads right up to this book. Doug Exley (superintendent, Gilbertsville-Mt. Upton), Karen Volpe, and the entire GMU staff have been wonderful colleagues—GMU is a very special small rural school community. Louis Wool (superintendent, Harrison), Louise Cleveland, and the many teachers I've come to know and respect at Harrison have challenged me to think more deeply about K–12 literacy. And I must thank Robert Roelle, Phyllis Glassman, Ray Sanchez, Mirla Puello, and Zoila Tazi, along with all the administrators, literacy coaches, and teachers with whom I've been working in Ossining Union Free School District. They have implemented the framework in ways that I would never have thought possible. In extending the framework downwards to birth, I am indebted to Lynnette Pannucci and her staff at the Rensselaer County Even Start; Mary Haust and Margaret Hoose; Cindy Gallagher and Dee Dwyer at New York State Education Department; and Chris Dwyer at RMC. They have all significantly enlarged my understanding of family literacy and the critical contributions it makes to K–12 language arts.

Add to this list Deborah Gregory, Larry Scanlon, Barney Sturm, Richard Booth, Elizabeth Brinkerhoff, Deb Sperling, Irene Press, Alan Pole, Marki Clair-O'Rourke, Jessica Cohen, Carol Exley, and Margaret Dwyer, all of whom have profoundly influenced my thinking and many of whose ideas have been incorporated into the framework.

Special thanks need to go to Lynnette Pannucci, Trudy Walp, and Jason Kinard for their thoughtful comments on earlier drafts of the book, and to Sue Bender and Dick Wilkinson for their support and wonderful company during some difficult times. Much of the manuscript was written in Saratoga Public Library, an ideal place in which to write and think.

I am also indebted to colleagues in the field who reviewed the manuscript for Jossey-Bass; their input was invaluable in making the final revisions. Lastly, I must thank Christie Hakim, my editor at Jossey-Bass, for her insights and encouragement; Cathy Mallon, who has shepherded the book to publication; and to Shana Harrington and Natalie Lin for their expert attention to the details of the manuscript and its publication.

About the Author

Sean Walmsley is professor and chair of the Reading Department, State University of New York at Albany. Born and raised in England, he graduated from Trinity College, Dublin, with his bachelor's and master's degrees in history, and from Harvard University with his Ed.D. in reading. He has several years teaching experience in elementary and secondary schools in both England and the United States.

Walmsley has published numerous articles in professional journals and has written several books related to language arts. He is author of *Children Exploring Their World: Theme Teaching in Elementary School* (Heinemann, 1994) and is coauthor with Bonnie Brown Walmsley of *Kindergarten: A Developmentally-Appropriate Approach* (Heinemann, 1992), *Kindergarten: Ready or Not?* (Heinemann, 1996), and *Teaching with Favorite Marc Brown Books* (Scholastic, 1998). He is coeditor, with Richard Allington, of *No Quick Fix: Rethinking Literacy Programs in America's Elementary Schools* (TC Press/IRA, 1995/2007).

For the past twenty-five years, Walmsley has worked closely with public schools, helping them rethink language arts instruction K–12, and is a popular workshop leader and speaker at conferences across the United States. For the past ten years, he has also focused on literacy issues from birth through pre-K, working in collaboration with colleagues from Even Start, a federally funded program to support literacy among the nation's poorest families.

Walmsley is a keen gardener and in his spare time is president of the Walmsley Society—a literary society in England devoted to the life and work of his father, the novelist Leo Walmsley, and his grandfather, Ulric Walmsley, the painter, both from Robin Hood's Bay in Yorkshire. His next project is building a passive-solar house.

Closing the Circle

Preamble: Rethinking Literacy Expectations

I could see that Mary, a second-grade teacher, wasn't happy with the way things were going. "We have a perfectly good language arts curriculum," she said, "and it lays out all the skills to be covered at each grade level. Why do we have to reinvent the wheel?"

I had been working with Mary and several of her colleagues in the summer of 1986, or thereabouts, to help her district in western Massachusetts bring its language arts curriculum up-to-date. The language arts committee was trying to articulate what we wanted children to look like as readers and *then* worry about what skills we needed to teach at each grade level. But Mary was adamant. Finally, I said to her, "Mary, can you bring in the curriculum guide, so we can look at it?" Mary disappeared, and about twenty minutes later returned with a fat binder that looked like it had sat on a back shelf for several years. She passed it around the group. No one else had seen it before. Mary explained that it had been compiled about five years previously by a language arts committee, working with a professor from a local college. As I leafed through its pages, I could see literally hundreds of skills, neatly handwritten, with columns to indicate the grade level at which each skill was to be introduced, when it was to be mastered, and when it needed to be reinforced. After everyone had had a chance to look at the binder, I casually asked Mary if she used the document for daily lesson planning. "Actually, no I don't," she said a little sheepishly. "In fact, I had a hard time finding it." Interesting, I thought. Here's a document that Mary insists should be the basis for the language arts curriculum—one that she herself had worked on—yet she doesn't even use it in her classroom.

Over the years, I've noticed something else about these lists of skills. Recently, I interviewed a sixth-grade teacher as part of a K–12 language arts "audit." She complained bitterly about students coming to her with poor spelling and grammar: "Why don't they teach them these in the elementary school? I have to spend the first month or so re-teaching the fifth-grade curriculum!" Later that day, I talked to a seventh-grade teacher in the same building. What was his complaint? You guessed it: no one had taught the students spelling and grammar in the sixth grade. So I went back to the sixth-grade teacher and asked first just how many students had poor spelling and grammar (about 10 percent) when they arrived in sixth grade, and how many still had spelling and grammar problems when they left (the same 10 percent).

I wondered why it hadn't occurred to her that what she expected the previous teacher to accomplish was the same thing the next teacher expected of her, yet she didn't expect this of herself. She had no better success with this 10 percent than either her predecessor or her successor. The lesson: even when teachers agree on which skills are to be taught at each grade level, there's no guarantee that these skills will be taught to mastery. In some states (Louisiana, for example), with the new emphasis on skills mastery, students have to learn their grade-level skills or else they don't go on to the next grade. Although this may be what the teacher at the next grade level has been asking for, it isn't what the teacher at the current grade wants to be held responsible for. When I shared these anecdotes at conferences or in workshops, I could see that they resonated with educators, yet no one seemed to pay much attention to the underlying problems with defining language arts as simply a list of skills. But as my misgivings grew, I started to think there must be a better way.

That better way came in 1987. I got a call from an old friend, Dick Leadem, with whom I'd worked in an alternative junior high school in Arlington, Massachusetts, when I was in the doctoral program at Harvard. Dick was the guidance counselor in Arlington and had since become principal at Manchester Elementary School, in Manchester Center, Vermont. Dick wanted to know if I'd be interested in helping his K–8 faculty rethink their reading program. What we set out to do was to articulate what we thought a student should look like as a reader as he or she left the eighth grade. What seemed like a pretty easy task ended up taking nearly two years to accomplish, but the exercise itself gave me the idea that describing in plain, simple English what attributes we wanted a student to possess as a reader was much better than listing all the reading skills we wanted to teach and the student to learn— especially if no one actually intended to teach them all and, if taught, no one could guarantee that the student would actually be a good reader.

Since that time, I have doggedly pursued this idea, and with the help of countless teachers and administrators in a variety of schools—mostly in New York State—the idea has grown into a framework for language arts that stretches from pre-K through grade 12. Recently, with support from colleagues in Even Start, I have extended the framework downward to birth.

Disconnections in Language Arts

I never set out to create a new framework for language arts, but my frustration with the way language arts is organized and delivered across grades K–12 has been steadily mounting over the past twenty-five years. As I've worked with rural, urban, and suburban school districts on various aspects of their literacy programs, I've come to realize that it's the whole framework, not just the individual bits and pieces, that so urgently needs rethinking. In other words, it isn't just about curriculum, or assessment, or expectations, but all of these, especially the connections among them.

First, if you look at the way language arts is organized and taught across the grades, you quickly realize how disconnected it is—disconnected in terms of the integration of reading, writing, and other language arts, disconnected in terms of language arts across the grade levels, and disconnected in terms of the relationship between language arts and content areas. I've often referred to language arts programs as yearlong "field trips" in which students engage in literacy activities created by classroom teachers, with little regard to what students have experienced before or what they're going to experience afterward. The disconnections apply up and down the grades, but they also occur among regular classroom language arts instruction, content-area instruction, instructional support, and programs for gifted and talented students. What's missing in almost all the schools I've observed or worked with is an articulation of the big picture—how all these various individual components (expectations, curriculum, assessment, reporting) are supposed to fit together.

Second, I'm increasingly concerned about what counts as literacy in schools. There's always been an emphasis on reading in America's elementary schools. For a decade, starting in the mid-1980s, the Whole Language movement made a determined effort to better balance reading with writing, speaking, and listening. But the last few years have seen a widespread retreat not just back to reading but to decoding skills—an essential component of reading fluency but neither the goal of reading nor even the most important aspect of it. A definition of reading has to include comprehension as well as decoding, and it has to include the understanding of big ideas, not just literal comprehension. Further, a definition of literacy has to include all the traditional components (reading, writing, speaking, listening), but it also needs to encompass *viewing* (making sense of what is observed) and *representing* (expressing ideas in a variety of media, not just in writing). Schools seem to have a hard time maintaining this balance, principally, I believe, because they don't have an overarching framework to guide them. So they bounce back and forth between emphases, swayed by what's popular or what state or federal government officials think ought to be emphasized.

The challenge of balancing language arts components, as well as aligning expectations, curriculum, assessment, and reporting, makes a new framework necessary. One of No Child Left Behind's (NCLB) greatest strengths has been its attempt to align expectations, curriculum, assessment, and reporting. One of its greatest shortcomings is its narrow view of literacy. Focusing primarily on reading components makes it easier to align everything, but it shortchanges students in terms of what they need to become fully literate. Indeed, early indications are that the results of NCLB—arguably the most invasive federal literacy initiative ever imposed on public schools—are very disappointing (Lee 2006; Fuller, Wright et al. 2007). I suspect that when the dust clears, the narrow focus on the decoding aspects of reading will emerge as a prime cause for its failure. What needs aligning is not one or two components but all of them. Most public schools come nowhere close to aligning all these components. They'll have literacy expectations, but often these are either poorly represented in the curricula across the grades or inadequately communicated in the report cards. Because what gets reported tends to define the expectations, it's the report card that often better reflects both the expectations and the literacy curriculum.

Difficulty of Long-Term Planning

I do not underestimate the challenge of implementing a new framework, especially one that attempts to represent all the language arts and span not just K–12 but also birth through pre-K. In proposing a new framework, I am well aware that it, too, may suffer the same fate as frameworks that have preceded it. In one district, I vividly recall a reading teacher at one of our first meetings. She asked, "What evidence can you provide us that if we adopt this approach, our test scores will go up?" Another teacher asked, "Why is this approach better than the one we've been working on these past few years and just abandoned?" I'm not sure exactly how I responded to these questions at the time, but here's how I'd respond now:

First, no one can guarantee that any framework or model will produce the desired results. There are simply too many variables over which neither teachers nor school districts have control. Districts have a long-standing reputation for not taking a long-term view of reform, which is fully justified, given how short the tenure of senior administrators is these days. In southern New York State, for example, the average tenure of a superintendent is now three to four years. Yet any serious school reform takes at least three times that long. Further, as I have experienced several times, districts tend to tire of any reform that lasts more than a year, and even if they don't abandon ones already in motion, they are quite willing to start up new ones without a thought about how the new reforms interact with the existing ones. I'm frequently asked by districts to sort out problems in language arts, only to find that the long-suffering teachers have three or four overlapping and unrelated programs they have to use in the time that only accommodates one.

A second issue is that "desired results" frequently means the results of state or federally mandated assessments. If a district sets out to prepare students to become fully literate, but the desired results are on tests that measure, say, just decoding skills, then many of the district's goals go unmeasured, and worse, enormous pressure builds up to refocus the curriculum on what's measured in the tests. In this environment, a framework that takes the larger, longer view of literacy will surely fail. Well, it may fail in the short term, but because its goals relate to genuine literacy, it may well succeed in its objectives anyway. But who will notice?

As will be seen throughout this book, I accept the reality of the tension between short- and long-term goals and between doing well on tests and preparing students well for the real world. I also understand that even though it would be good if districts undertook long-term reforms, any new framework that can only succeed with a ten- to fifteen-year commitment is not a viable proposition in the current educational climate.

So what would I offer as a rationale for the framework I propose in this book?

An Operational Framework

First, the framework is fully operational. I have worked with a number of school districts over the years, and although many of them have, primarily for reasons given earlier, abandoned the approach, they have nonetheless both contributed to the viability of the framework and profited from it. I would offer two districts—one rural and one suburban—that have had all the components in place, K–6, for at least three years. In Harrison Central School District in Westchester County, New York, the framework is fully implemented, K–8, with ongoing work to implement it in grades 9–12. In Gilbertsville-Mt. Upton, a small rural school near Oneonta, New York, the framework has been in place, K–6, since 2000, and there is ongoing work to implement it in grades 7–8 and beyond.

Other districts have parts of the framework in place (for example, report cards are aligned with literacy attributes in Oneonta City School District, New York, and in Cairo-Durham, in the Catskills, New York; Brewster County School District in New York has literacy attributes and non-negotiable contributions in place, but further development has been held up by a change in administration). The most recent project is Ossining, New York, which has literacy programs from birth through grade 12. Here the framework is being implemented with commitment to a long-range implementation. Finally, the framework has been implemented in an Even Start program (Rensselaer County Family Literacy Partnership, New York). This project is where the birth–pre-K attributes (non-negotiables) have been developed. Although it is true that no systematic research has yet been conducted in these sites to show the effectiveness of the framework on test results, in most cases, it's too early to demonstrate what these effects are. However, the districts appear to be well satisfied with both the framework itself and the effectiveness of its implementation.

Second, the framework is not tied to a particular language arts instructional philosophy or program. It will work with or without a basal reading series. It is as effective in a district with a strong commitment to whole language as one that emphasizes direct instruction in basic literacy skills. It is highly suited to "mixed" approaches, which is typical of most public schools. However, it challenges instructional approaches that don't fully support literacy expectations. So language arts instruction and experiences that fail to address all components of literacy would need to be revised. For example, the framework insists that attention be paid to critical, as well as literal, comprehension. It would also insist that writing not be shortchanged (or, conversely, overdone) at the expense of other aspects of language arts. But the framework is neutral with respect to curriculum materials. It doesn't require or proscribe any specific materials, whether commercial or "homegrown." The ultimate test of any approach or materials would be that students acquire their district's literacy attributes.

Third, the framework offers a principled approach to articulating language arts expectations. The literacy attributes (our expectations for what we want a student to know, do, understand, and have experienced in language arts, K–12) are few in number but cover all components of language arts; they also represent the most important objectives. Further, unlike any other approach of which I am aware, they span across not only K–12 but also birth through pre-K. What this accomplishes is a clear, simple set of literacy expectations that are easily understood by educators and the lay public, are common to all grade levels, and provide consistency throughout elementary, middle, and high school. Further, they provide parents and early childhood providers with a set of literacy expectations that are appropriate for infants and toddlers, yet are aligned with school expectations. At a time when increasing numbers of children come to school inadequately prepared for literacy, having a framework that covers birth through grade 12 puts a district and its community at a distinct advantage.

Fourth, the framework articulates a simple, clear approach to aligning expectations, curriculum, instructional support, assessment, reporting, and data analysis. In most school districts, most of these elements are not only unaligned; they frequently conflict with one another. For example, notice how many schools have report cards that don't match the curriculum, let alone the district's language arts expectations. Others have aligned some of these components, but this framework aligns all of them.

Fifth, the framework offers a set of *non-negotiable instructional contributions* that are implemented through *instructional activities*. The non-negotiables are what each and every educator needs to provide students, based on research and best practice. The non-negotiables ensure, for example, that there's consistency of coverage across the grades, yet allow room for teachers to differentiate instruction for students who need it, through instructional activities that carry out the non-negotiables. This dual approach respects, values, and draws on teachers' unique abilities and strengths in how to provide appropriate experiences for learners. It is a novel and effective way to tread that difficult path between letting teachers "do their own thing," which results in highly inconsistent practice, and micromanaging instructional practices that make teachers feel and act like robots.

Sixth, a district wouldn't have to fully buy into the framework in order to profit from it. In working with many schools over the past twenty years, I have seen them profit from engaging with the framework without completely embracing it. For example, the clarity that comes from articulating the few, really important literacy expectations helps a district with just that one task, even if it doesn't use other elements of the framework. Or using the framework's strategy of aligning the report cards with the literacy expectations can be done independently of anything else. In this case, making the report card reflect progress toward the district's expectations rather than simply progress in the curriculum (not the same thing, as I explain later) will be very helpful. Or a district could use the framework to ensure that every important literacy expectation is kept track of and reported.

Even if a district were to focus all its efforts on raising test scores, the framework could be used to accomplish that task.

Although it would involve narrowing the literacy expectations a great deal more than I would advocate, the framework could be used very effectively to this end. Of course, I would argue that a language arts curriculum that does cover all components and consistently addresses them across the grades will produce good test scores. It will also produce students with strong language abilities and experiences. However, I can understand why districts have narrowed their focus in recent years, as high-stakes measures of narrowly defined literacy skills dominate the educational landscape.

Seventh, although the framework focuses on language arts, there is no reason why it cannot be used to articulate expectations, curriculum, and assessment in other curriculum areas. Although I do not currently have projects that explore this use, several districts have expressed interest in it. In Gilbertsville-Mt. Upton, teachers working on report cards have adopted many of the framework's principles to articulate appropriate assessments and report card categories for science and social studies. Teachers in other districts have used the framework to focus their math instruction on what really matters to them. However, I do not report on these in my book.

Finally, amid the repeated calls for a national literacy curriculum, I would offer an attributes framework as a viable candidate. My colleague Dick Allington has said that elementary schools already have a national curriculum called basal reading series (Allington 2002). Others call for nationwide adoption of so-called scientifically based reading materials. Neither basal reading series nor packaged literacy materials, however "scientific" they may be, can be considered a curriculum because they offer such narrow definitions of literacy. However, they are good candidates for instructional materials in support of a curriculum. An attributes framework *is* a language arts curriculum, and it provides the kind of balance and comprehensiveness that a national curriculum calls for.

1

A NEW LANGUAGE ARTS FRAMEWORK

I titled this book *Closing the Circle* in part be cause that's what I've done with the framework over the past twenty years. I started in Manchester Elementary (Manchester Center, Vermont) in the late 1980s with just one part of the framework—articulating literacy attributes—and ever since then, I've been filling in the rest of the circle. To be honest, I didn't even think of it as a circle until quite recently, but as each of the elements was added, it inevitably took on a circular shape.

The framework consists of a set of five related components:

1. *Literacy attributes* (clear, simple expectations we have for all students)

2. *Instructional contributions* (what instruction and experiences each grade level must provide in order for students to acquire the attributes, as well as what is needed to support struggling learners)

3. *Assessments* of students' progress toward the attributes (through a variety of informal and formal assessments)

4. *Reports* on students' progress toward the attributes (to parents via report cards and progress reports)

5. *Analysis of data* to inform instruction and to revise components of the framework

In this chapter, I'll provide a brief overview of each of these components but will first discuss some basic assumptions about the

Exhibit 1.1. A Framework for Language Arts.

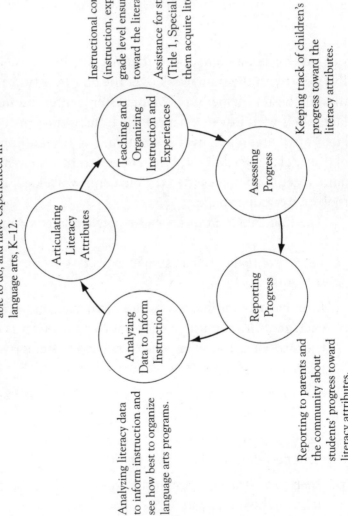

What we want children to know, be able to do, and have experienced in language arts, K–12.

Instructional contributions (instruction, experiences) at each grade level ensure steady progress toward the literacy attributes.

Assistance for struggling children (Title 1, Special Education) helps them acquire literacy attributes.

Keeping track of children's progress toward the literacy attributes.

Reporting to parents and the community about students' progress toward literacy attributes.

Analyzing literacy data to inform instruction and see how best to organize language arts programs.

Articulating Literacy Attributes

Teaching and Organizing Instruction and Experiences

Assessing Progress

Reporting Progress

Analyzing Data to Inform Instruction

framework and explain the literacy philosophy that undergirds it. Exhibit 1.1 shows a graphic representation of the framework.

Basic Assumptions

The framework rests on some basic assumptions about what counts as literacy and how the various components are related to one another. A language arts curriculum has to address all aspects of both receptive and expressive literacy, and it has to rest on a solid theoretical foundation.

What Counts as Literacy?

I have always been puzzled by the terminology used to define and describe what counts as literacy. Of course, it doesn't help matters when the world's most respected professional organization devoted to literacy is called the International Reading Association (IRA), and my own department at the University at Albany is called the Reading Department. Further, the terms *English/language arts*, and *reading/language arts* are still in common use, seemingly to distinguish between *English*, *reading*, and *language arts*. Throw in *language* and *literacy*, and no wonder there's confusion!

For early childhood educators, especially, the term *language* refers to listening and speaking and often is distinguished from *literacy* by thinking about these as prerequisites for reading and writing. *English* is traditionally the term used for the study of literature at the secondary level, with *language arts* as an equivalent term for elementary schools. *Reading* typically refers to what teachers emphasize in the very early grades, and the term has also been used in remedial classrooms, as in *remedial reading* or *struggling readers*. Yet the use of the term *reading* definitely implies its greater importance as one of the language arts, which is why I think the term *reading/language arts* is still very common. The problem with adopting the term *literacy* to cover all of these is that for a long time it was associated with adults or with the United Nations, and it was hard to untangle from these connections. Since Marie Clay (Clay 1972) coined the term *emergent literacy* to describe the development of very young children and to replace the outdated term and notion of *reading readiness*, the term *literacy* has become acceptable to encompass all aspects of language arts, even from the very earliest beginnings. And even if the IRA has resisted changing its name (and our department is still called Reading), there's no question that neither is exclusively concerned with reading. So for me, the term *literacy* is the right word to use when we are talking about language, reading, English, or language arts. It covers them all.

I define *literacy* within the two major areas of receptive and expressive literacy. *Receptive literacy* is all about understanding "texts" (or utterances, gestures, drawings, and so on) that originate with others and are either read, heard, or viewed. *Expressive literacy* is all about creating and communicating meaning through writing, speaking, and other media (for example, drawing or illustrating, dramatic playacting, making multimedia presentations, modeling, or playing music). No one has to be persuaded that reading, writing, speaking, and listening are important components of language arts, although, traditionally, reading has been considered the most important. Writing is a close second; speaking and listening trail behind; viewing and representing are barely represented.

See Exhibit 1.2 for a graphical representation of my definition of literacy.

For a decade or so, starting in the mid-1980s, the Whole Language movement gave reading, writing, speaking, and listening

Exhibit 1.2. What Is Literacy?

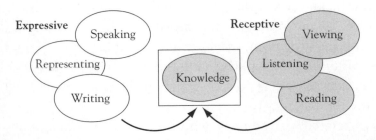

much more equitable attention (Harste, Short et al. 1987). It also emphasized the notion of literary understanding (as opposed to just reading comprehension) in the early grades—an aspect of literacy that traditionally had largely been confined to the middle and high school. Since the late 1990s, and especially with the passage of No Child Left Behind legislation in 2001, reading has again been thrust into the foreground, with decoding given a prominence it hasn't had in decades.

One of the purposes of this book is to advocate a return to a more balanced and inclusive definition of *literacy* and *language arts*.

Viewing and representing have never been major components of the nation's public schools, but they have been elsewhere, and they are both included in the joint professional standards of the National Council of Teachers of English (NCTE) and the IRA. For example:

- Students read a wide range of print and non-print texts to build an understanding of texts, of themselves, and of the cultures of the United States and the world. . . .
- Students use spoken, written, and visual language to accomplish their own purposes (e.g., for learning, enjoyment, persuasion, and the exchange of information).

I also learned recently that viewing and representing have been components of Canada's definition of literacy since at least the 1950s. Viewing and "presenting" (that's what New Zealanders call representing) are components of New Zealand's definition, too.

There are persuasive arguments for including viewing and representing in a definition of language arts. One is that very young children initially acquire what they know about the world through viewing and listening, prior to making sense of it through reading. Similarly, they communicate with the world through representations (gestures, facial expressions, cries, laughter, movements) and speaking, prior to their ability to write. Reading has its origins in viewing; writing originates in other forms of representation.

Another is that literacy in the real world has become more visual in the past twenty years, with the advent of the Internet and with the creation of tools such as desktop publishing that put representational skills into the hands of ordinary people. Who, twenty years ago, would have thought that an ordinary mortal, with no more than simple computer skills, could take digital photographs at a wedding, remove all the red spots, crop the pictures, and within an hour or so have them up on a Web site for all to see?

It's interesting, too, to see how important representation is in the "real" world outside of school. You see this every day in newspapers, magazines, and in Web sites. It is especially evident in museums, where a great deal of thought goes into sharing discoveries or conveying knowledge in ways that challenge viewers to examine them from different—and often conflicting—perspectives.

It's no secret that literacy is shedding its preoccupation with text as it dons increasingly digital clothing. Distasteful as this might be to educators and parents wedded to a textual definition of literacy, the world that awaits our current elementary and secondary students both demands and rewards those who can make sense of what they see, as well as read, and can express themselves in a variety of media, not just in writing and in speech.

For these reasons, I argue that receptive literacy should include reading, listening, and *viewing* and that expressive literacy should include writing, speaking, and *representing*. Of course, reading is a form of viewing, but viewing encompasses much more than reading. Similarly, writing is a form of representation, but writing is only one of many ways to represent what one wants to share with others.

How Do the Components of Literacy Interact?

At the heart of this framework is what's called the *communication triangle*, the origins of which can be found in Aristotle and which forms the foundation for the literacy field (Kinneavy 1970). Simply stated, the communication triangle represents the basic relationships among those who *create and express ideas* (writers, speakers, representers), those who *receive and make sense* of them (readers, listeners, and viewers), the *topics or ideas* themselves, and the *actual text* (or utterance, or representation). All of these interactions lie within a social context that influences—in some cases, controls—these interactions.

But the communication triangle doesn't simply describe the players. It also suggests how they can—and should—interact in ways that support growth in expressive and receptive language. Moffett, for example, in *Teaching the Universe of Discourse* (Moffett 1967), argues that a writer (or speaker, or representer, for that matter) develops greater control of writing through written compositions that put increasing distance between the writer and audience, have different purposes (for example, expressive, informational, persuasive), range across a variety of topics, and require increasing control of style and language. Similarly, readers (or listeners, or viewers) develop greater understanding through engagement with texts (utterances, non-print material) that range across topics and purposes and represent increasing complexity of ideas and syntax.

See Exhibit 1.3 for a graphical representation of the *communication triangle*.

More recently, the notion of a social context surrounding all communicative acts has made us realize that certain conventions define and constrain the kinds of communications that typically occur, the ways that language is used, and what counts as appropriate or correct. Thus within the social context of a home, language that's informal and assumes a great amount of shared knowledge is appropriate. However, within the social context of a school, language that's more formal and has to abide by the conventions of school or a state's academic discourse is expected. These conventions vary from one content area or grade to another, but they are different from what's typical at home and what's expected in other social contexts, such as in college or in business.

One way to illustrate how the social context works is to see it in action. Almost every American child has, at some point in upper-elementary school, done the "peanut-butter-and-jelly" exercise. It seems to be a rite of passage. Unless a child has just stepped off a plane from England, he or she already knows what

Exhibit 1.3. Components of Literacy.

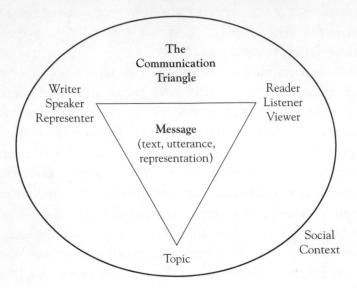

a PBJ looks like and almost certainly knows how to construct one. But no matter—this exercise is to explain, precisely, how to make a PBJ and then have a classmate carry out the instructions. The recipient of the instructions typically fails, because the instruction giver has omitted some essential step (for example, forgetting to take the bread out of the plastic wrapping or not opening the drawer to select a knife). Although it's a fun activity, it's also a sober reminder of the social context at work. In the real world of home, there are so many shared understandings about everyday kitchen objects and groceries that giving instructions for making a PBJ doesn't need to include things like taking the bread out of the wrapper or opening a kitchen drawer to pick out a knife to spread the PB and J. It's precisely *because* children know this familiar social context that when asked to supply precise instructions, they omit the obvious while focusing on the essentials. So the child who describes the process appropriately ("you take two slices of bread, and on one slice spread some peanut butter, and on the other spread your favorite jam, and then slap the two together") is penalized, while the one who fully understands the literalness of the task starts by describing in excruciating detail how to extract the bread from its wrapper and the knife from the kitchen drawer gets to be the Student of the Week.

More seriously, the social context constantly defines and redefines the content and form of communicative engagement, and it requires students to be flexible and adaptable, as one context insists on Modern Languages Association (MLA) as the basis for bibliographies, while another requires the American Psychological Association (APA). From adhering to the format of a friendly letter in second grade, to creating a PowerPoint presentation in twelfth grade, to writing a college research paper, and eventually preparing a report for an advertising agency, or even designing an exhibit in a major museum, the social context frames what's acceptable in terms of content, style and language, and format. Thus although a graduate student *could* submit a term paper in the form of a friendly letter, that's not likely to be acceptable. Conversely, giving an academic talk in a gathering of lay folk doesn't work, either. I once attended an amateur society devoted to a regional author in England, only to find half the audience falling asleep as they tried to listen to an overly academic talk on the writer's style. The identical talk in a university setting would surely not have met the same fate.

Learning what is acceptable is very much part of becoming a successful language user. However, what's acceptable depends on the context, and it changes over time, so good readers and writers need to be adaptable, too. In other words, there's a constant interplay between literacy practices themselves and the social context in which literacy practices occur. For example, although many traditional educators rail against the use of abbreviations (for example, LOL for Laugh Out Loud) in instant messaging, the abbreviations themselves have their origins in painfully manipulating tiny buttons on a cell phone to create text. Changes in typesetting and advances in graphic design have seriously challenged traditional ways of writing business letters so that what children are taught in school is often completely anachronistic.

Of course, the social context doesn't merely define "acceptable" discourse; it also privileges particular ways of engaging in literacy and demeans or discourages other ways. So the notion that the social context is benign has to be constantly challenged and guarded against—a topic I'll return to in Chapter Two.

Elements of the Framework

The framework comprises five major elements: (1) *literacy attributes*, which represent the common set of language arts expectations, preschool through grade 12; (2) *non-negotiable instructional contributions and instructional activities* in regular classrooms and support programs; (3) *assessments* that keep track of students' progress toward the attributes; (4) *reports* that communicate progress to parents, schools, and community, and (5) *analysis of data* to inform and improve instruction. In the sections that follow, I'll briefly explain each of the components.

Literacy Attributes

Attributes represent what we want a student to know, do, understand, and have experienced in language arts. Attributes include literacy skills (for example, strategies for figuring out unknown words), but they also embrace literacy practices such as reading widely. Attributes, as I define them, are the most important characteristics of an accomplished literate person in the twenty-first century—someone we would regard as proficient as a reader, writer, speaker, listener, viewer, and representer; with extensive background knowledge; and one who practices literacy, rather than just knowing how to.

Literacy attributes come from several sources:

- Professional standards (for example, NCTE, IRA, and the NAEYC, or the National Association for the Education of Young Children)

- State English/Language Arts Standards and assessments
- Professional and research literature in the literacy field
- Literacy expectations of teachers, specialists, administrators, parents, and members of the school community

Attributes represent what we want a student to be able to do and to have experienced across the grades, so they are different from the traditional listing of language arts skills at each grade level. There are serious problems with these traditional grade-level skills.

First, listing them by grade level, especially in terms of mastery, wrongly assumes that literacy learning progresses by the calendar.

Second, there's more to literacy development than the acquisition of skills. For example, consider the attribute "reads widely." Reading widely is not a literacy skill. It's a literacy experience. Yet it is both a critical contributor to literacy skills and an important goal of learning to read. By focusing on skills (and far too many of them—in my children's elementary school, there were typically 200–300 skills listed per grade level), important aspects of language arts are given short shrift.

Third, if skills are listed by grade level, there's a tendency to create new skills at different grade levels, if only to differentiate among the grades. For example, the difference between understanding informational text in grade 1 and grade 12 is that the informational text itself becomes conceptually and syntactically more dense. The actual strategies needed to make sense of text remain constant. Making text-to-text or text-to-self connections works just as effectively in kindergarten as in secondary school.

An attribute approach differs in several important ways. First, it lists only the few, really important literacy expectations. Very few teachers can (or do) keep 200–300 skills in their head while teaching a grade level. But they can keep 10–15 critical expectations in mind. By "tucking in" the smaller skills and expectations underneath the attributes, not only does the list become more manageable; it also ensures that what's critical is on top, while the supporting details are folded underneath. This helps everyone focus on what matters, and it ensures that the language arts curriculum doesn't substitute smaller for larger goals, trivial ones for those more important.

Second, attributes reflect our expectations for students across a significant time period (preschool through grade 12, at least), so they aren't listed by grade level. This has both an upside and a downside. The upside is that we are freed from the constraint of having to lay out an entire set of expectations for each grade level. By doing this, we avoid creating artificial distinctions between, say, reading comprehension strategies at different grade levels. More important, we can maintain a consistent focus on the few critical expectations across the grades.

However, the biggest advantage of this approach is that it doesn't assume or require that students acquire literacy attributes on a chronological schedule. So a child age three who reads fluently doesn't have to be put on hold until second grade. He can simply progress to other literacy attributes. Similarly, a student who is in seventh grade but cannot read fluently still has that as an expectation, despite her age and grade placement. The downside is that some of the attributes are not suitable for students in particular grade levels, either because they can only be acquired by very few children or because they no longer apply to the vast majority. For example, the attribute "reads fluently" would not be appropriate as an expectation for all but a handful of three- or four-year-olds; conversely, it wouldn't be appropriate for almost all students beyond grade 3 who can read fluently. (Of course, it depends on how "reads fluently" is defined. I'll get to that presently.) Most attributes, however, will apply equally to preschoolers and secondary students, provided that they are qualified by the expression *appropriate*—appropriate with respect to the conceptual density of the content or the complexity of the form, or both. Also, once one of these attributes has been acquired, it can be dropped as an expectation for individual students. This notion will become clearer, as I explain the concept of instructional contributions and especially so when I get to assessment.

Third, attributes are expressed in plain, simple, language so that everyone—students, parents, educators, and the lay public—can relate to them. This isn't an easy task, but it's necessary. "Demonstrates awareness of the alphabetic principle" typically wouldn't be an attribute, partly because it's too specific (it needs to be tucked inside "reads fluently" or "decodes fluently") but also because it's too technical.

Fourth, attributes are intended to represent language arts expectations not just for school but also for life-long learning, critical thinking, and informed, active participation in our American democracy, as well as in a global economy. A child who is currently in kindergarten will almost certainly graduate under a different set of state and federal language arts standards than are currently in effect for secondary students. So keeping an eye on the future, especially beyond formal schooling, is an important task in creating expectations. This is not an easy undertaking. I well remember thinking in the 1980s that the Internet, at that time a clumsy and hugely difficult mechanism for communicating between universities, would ultimately go nowhere. It never occurred to me then that it would transform almost every aspect of communication, let alone broaden the very definition of literacy.

Finally, while meeting or exceeding standards on state examinations is a very important goal for school literacy, the attributes go much further than that. Students who possess the attributes will do well on state examinations, but they will also be well equipped for the literacy challenges of work, careers, and life.

Non-Negotiable Instructional Contributions

All the years I have been observing and working in public school classrooms have made me realize that what most students do across the grade levels is engage in a series of yearlong "field trips" with teachers, with mini-excursions to specialists, depending on whether they are academically talented or struggling with basic literacy or numeracy skills. When I use the term *field trip*, what I mean is that students enter a classroom in September and are taken on an educational journey for a year in the company of a teacher, who has considerable control over where that journey goes, what's included or not included, and whether what's taught builds on what's been done before or relates to what is coming ahead. Sarason (1991) notes how isolated teachers are from one another. They spend much of their days in the company of little people (students), with very little time to interact with other adults. For the same reason, their entire language arts curriculum is often isolated from other grade levels. I frequently hear from teachers that they really know little about what happens in other grades, and sometimes when they talk about other grade levels, I know for a fact that their perceptions are wrong.

The more I delve into this, the more I'm convinced that the field-trip metaphor dominates the thinking and practice of language arts instruction across the grades. Another example: in schools where samples of student work are passed along from grade to grade (these become a storage nightmare by the time they reach middle school!), I find that most teachers want their students' work to be passed on, but they are not particularly interested in what comes to them from previous grades. I've asked teachers about this, and they tell me that (1) they like students to start off with a clean slate, and (2) they don't need anyone else to tell them where a student is; they can tell that within a few days of the student arriving in their class.

I want to propose here that the field-trip metaphor be replaced by the notion of *instructional contributions*, so that instead of a student embarking on what is essentially a grade-level excursion under the guidance and control of a classroom teacher, the year-long experience in language arts is instead a set of instructional contributions toward the acquisition of the literacy attributes.

Definition of Instructional Contributions. Before I go any further, I need to explain what I mean by *instructional contributions*. I mean everything that goes on in classrooms (and what goes on outside it, too, directed or encouraged by teachers) throughout the school year that supports students' acquisition of the attributes. Contributions include instruction and experiences. By *instruction* I mean teaching skills and strategies—directly or indirectly or in combination; by *experiences*, I mean all the activities that teachers engage students in (for example, independent reading and writing, read-alouds, dramatic play, reader's theater, and field trips). We are currently in a period where direct, explicit instruction is seen by some as the most important element in literacy teaching. I don't doubt the necessity of direct instruction where it's needed and especially when it unlocks literacy difficulties among struggling students. However, the contribution of what Donald Holdaway calls *incidental learning*—learning that occurs along the way, in "teachable moments," in places and at times when what is learned isn't the focus of instruction, is not to be discounted (Holdaway 1979). Nor is what I call *sustained engagement*, which is what happens when teachers intentionally engage students in appropriate literacy experiences over a long period of time.

One way of characterizing instructional contributions is to differentiate between direct and indirect instruction. But I think a more useful distinction is between what I call *non-negotiable contributions* that represent instruction and experiences that every teacher and specialist must provide all students and *instructional activities* that implement the non-negotiables. The idea is that when each educator implements these non-negotiables, all students will make the best possible progress toward the attributes. The non-negotiable contributions represent the "equal educational opportunities" provided to every student; they employ best practices that come from research, the professional literature, and the collective experience and wisdom of professional educators. Non-negotiables also provide the sustained engagement in core literacy activities needed not only to ensure consistency within and across grades but also to ensure that students have had sufficient exposure to and participation in what they need to become fully literate. I sometimes wonder if students were consistently engaged in literacy activities across a long period of time, whether so many of them would struggle so much and, consequently, have to receive supplementary support that, ironically, often denies them the very opportunities (like independent reading) they need to overcome their difficulties. In fact, they might need fewer of these engagements in a given grade level, if only more grade levels provided the experiences.

Instructional Activities. *Instructional activities* are ones selected by individual teachers and specialists to implement the non-negotiables and thereby support students' progress toward the attributes. These activities represent the accommodations needed to address the particular strengths and needs of diverse students, as well as put to good use the craft and expertise of individual teachers. They also represent legitimately different instructional methods and materials to achieve common goals. Further, they provide the variety so necessary to motivate students across the years. Has anyone thought about how boring routines become when they are done year in and year out? When journal writing first hit the scene in the early 1980s, it was a refreshing alternative to the teacher-assigned topics of the 1960s and '70s. But soon it spread across elementary schools, and within a few years it wasn't quite so refreshing anymore. Children were ecstatic about journals when they first tried them. Recently, I've heard children groan when asked to get out their journals. I see the same thing happening with Post-it notes to assist children with reading comprehension strategies and with reader's and writer's workshop, especially if the formula for these activities is too rigid, and teachers are compelled to follow strict guidelines. But there's another reason to insist on flexibility of instructional activities while implementing the non-negotiables: it's to preserve and strengthen the professional knowledge of individual teachers.

To briefly describe how this works, let me share an example. "Reads widely" is an attribute; the non-negotiable instructional contributions might include

- Reads aloud frequently, choosing material from a wide range of sources (for example, genre, topic, forms of print).
- Provide regular opportunities, encouragement and support for students to read widely in and out of school.

These are *non-negotiable*. In other words, all teachers would have to read aloud to students, drawing their material from a wide range of sources. They would have to provide regular opportunities, encouragement, and support for students to read widely on their own. Non-negotiables don't specify the titles of books and other materials that make up the wide range of choices; neither do they specify how and when teachers will provide opportunities for students to read widely or the particular techniques needed to guide and support a given student. These are what I call the *instructional activities*. Of course, how negotiable these activities end up being really depends on the district and the school. Many districts are quite fearful that the concept of flexibility in instructional activities leads to teachers simply doing their own thing, yet often these are the very districts that advocate differentiated instruction. I see flexibility as necessary for differentiated instruction, as well as for tapping into teachers' pedagogical strengths. (Ironic, isn't it, that we talk so much about teaching to students' strengths but so rarely encourage teachers to teach from theirs.) So long as the non-negotiables are met, and students are making good progress toward the literacy attributes, no one should fear anarchy in the classroom. I have also noticed in many districts where teachers are required to all use the same commercial programs, there is so much variation that they might as well be doing their own thing.

There is one aspect of the instructional activities that I'll come back to in later chapters but is worth mentioning here. There is some merit in teachers within and across grade levels coming to consensus on some activities, where it can be shown that students profit from sustained exposure to specific teaching and learning techniques. One example might be to agree on using techniques from *Mosaic of Thought* (Keene and Zimmermann 1997) or *Nonfiction Matters* (Harvey 1998) over several grades, so that children become completely familiar with them. One of my concerns, however, is that not all children will find these techniques effective in developing their own comprehension strategies. The other is that, once instituted, a selected approach becomes hard to dislodge, even in the face of questionable results for some or many of the students.

Organization of Literacy Instruction. The framework recognizes that there are many ways to organize literacy instruction to best meet the attributes. It doesn't advocate any particular curriculum or organizational design, but it strenuously challenges approaches that fail to implement the non-negotiables or ignore any of the attributes.

For example, in a theme-based approach to language arts, students read, write, listen, speak, view, and represent within a content-rich, integrated framework. A genre approach focuses on one genre at a time. A workshop approach emphasizes reading or writing, or a combination of these. All these approaches are supported by this framework. The framework is also neutral with respect to commercial materials. It neither favors nor discourages particular programs, but it does challenge a program that fails to provide appropriate contributions to all of the literacy attributes. In these cases, modifications will be necessary to ensure that the non-negotiables are met. The framework also is neutral with respect to the allocation of time to language arts, as well as to the particular organizational structure of literacy instruction. However, the organization of language arts must allow teachers to fully implement the non-negotiables.

Literacy Across the Curriculum. The question always arises about how much of the contribution to the literacy attributes should be made within English/language arts, and how much from other subject areas. In a self-contained classroom, this is relatively easy to figure out, because the classroom teacher has control over the entire daily schedule for subjects taught within the classroom. In the upper-elementary, middle, and high schools, the challenge is quite different. Not only is less time available for English/language arts, but subject-area teachers have to cover their content and meet exacting requirements of state examinations. Yet contributions need to be made from across content areas if a student is to be fully literate in them—if they are to read, think, write, and represent like a scientist, mathematician, artist, musician, sports player, or historian; if they are to interpret primary source documents; if they are to acquire the background knowledge needed to make sense of more complex texts.

Traditionally, in the reading field, we have promoted the idea of content-area teachers becoming reading (and more recently, writing) teachers. In fact, in a school I observed recently, the art teacher was complaining that she had to increase the amount of reading and writing and decrease the artwork ("representation") in order to make this happen. Sad, isn't it, that the one place where representation in ways other than simply writing can flourish is the very place where it's being discouraged? Also, the art room might be the one place where a child who struggles with reading and writing can find alternate ways to acquire knowledge and express understanding. I've also seen this happening in music. No, content area teachers *shouldn't* be asked to become language arts specialists; rather, they should make contributions to language arts through deepening and extending students' understanding of their content, as well as by engaging students in reading, writing, speaking, listening, viewing, and representing that are intimately connected to the content areas.

Instructional Support. In the framework, all instructional support programs (for example, Special Education, Title 1) are aligned to both the attributes and to the regular classroom instructional contributions. However, they will necessarily go beyond regular instruction to ensure that all literacy needs are met. Ensuring that the literacy attributes are the starting and ending point for both regular instruction and instructional support is a critical requirement of this framework, as *all* students are expected to meet the same high English/Language Arts Standards.

It can be a struggle for schools to align instructional support with regular language arts programs. Part of the challenge is reconciling instructional philosophies. For example, behaviorist, or "bottom-up," approaches advocated by many special educators don't easily mix with constructivist approaches favored by many classroom teachers. It's not easy to align an instructional support program that insists on teaching reading subskills to mastery prior to engaging struggling readers in authentic text—or one that insists on having students master reading skills before engaging them in writing—or teaching them only writing mechanics while ignoring composition.

The situation has become even more complicated since the passage of No Child Left Behind and IDEA2004. These legislative acts not only emphasize reading over all other language arts components; they also emphasize decoding over all other aspects of reading. They also have forced classroom teachers to abandon constructivist teaching methods and replace them with behaviorist pedagogies.

I'll describe in more detail (see Chapter Four) how I think instructional support programs might best be integrated. Here let me just say that the best instructional support programs start with high-quality instructional contributions in the regular classroom, including targeted, differentiated instruction for struggling students. These contributions will need to be supplemented with additional support, including intensive, one-on-one instruction. But the goals remain the same: all students will acquire the literacy attributes. They may not acquire them at the same pace or in the same way, which is why we will always need instructional support programs. But if the goals are broad enough and accommodate a wide range of aspirations and expectations for what counts as being fully literate, the needs of struggling students will be addressed. Although everyone has jumped on the bandwagon of "high standards," if standards are defined too narrowly (for example, primarily academic, or job-related, or just literacy skills), then it will be inappropriate for everyone to be held to them.

Assessments

Several principles guide the literacy assessments in this framework:

- All assessments should relate to and provide information on each student's progress toward the literacy attributes.
- Assessments should be used primarily to inform and improve instruction.
- Assessments should be economical and, wherever possible, embedded within regular classroom instruction.
- Assessments should draw on observations, conversations, and analysis of samples of literacy behaviors, not just literacy tasks or tests.
- Formal literacy assessments should have best available reliability and validity.

Language arts programs need the best assessments we can find that tell us where our students are relative to the attributes, and this will inevitably mean mixing formal and informal measures, as well as ones that have good psychometric properties, with ones that may be wanting in some of these properties yet still provide useful information. Acknowledging the imperfections of all assessments is important, but this should not deter us from doing our best to say where each student is relative to the literacy attributes, so we can support students' progress toward them. We need to consider how often to assess students and how best we can integrate assessment with instruction. We also need to use a variety of measures (observation, conversation, formal and informal tasks, analysis of samples) to measure students' progress and status. Keeping assessments simple, unobtrusive, yet comprehensive and as valid as we can possibly make them is the key here.

Reports

In this framework, the elementary report cards need to provide parents with information about each student's current status in each of the literacy attributes. Report cards, therefore, have to be aligned with the attributes so that students' current status and growth toward them can be communicated. At the middle and secondary levels, reporting progress toward the attributes has to be considered alongside traditional grading practices that are required for college entry, as well as the constraints of class loads (secondary teachers frequently have over one hundred students, compared to twenty-five or so in elementary school). Whether this can best be accomplished through analyzing samples of student work—tasks that tap into different literacy attributes, interims, or self-assessments—remains to be explored.

Analysis of Data

Finally, in this framework, literacy assessment data are gathered across the grades and analyzed to support language arts planning. Two kinds of data are gathered: (1) assessment data that are used to complete the report cards and (2) data from districtwide or state-mandated testing. For example, in the early grades, teachers might be using the Developmental Reading Assessment (DRA) to determine each student's reading fluency level, along with measures of phonemic awareness, letter and letter-sound identification, and so on. DRAs chart the progress students are making toward the attribute "decodes fluently." But the same data could be used to assess the contribution of individual aspects of fluency (for example, letter knowledge, phonemic awareness) on students' overall fluency (as measured by the DRA) and also toward reading comprehension. These data could also be analyzed to see which attributes are most highly correlated with meeting standards on state ELA examinations. For example, with students at risk of failure on the state examinations, is instruction and experience in some aspects of reading (for example, understanding big ideas, reading widely) more effective than instruction or experience in others (for example, "decodes fluently")? Data can also be used to make programmatic or organizational decisions. If the data from pre-K showed that students were unusually needy in, say, letter knowledge, providing additional support in both pre-K and kindergarten to address this need might be particularly beneficial. It might suggest a temporary reassignment of instructional support staff to support the pre-K and kindergarten teachers. If the data showed that children's knowledge of poetry was weak, this might point to gaps in teacher knowledge about poetry, which in turn could lead to targeted professional development.

Given a district's commitment to annual goals for student achievement (albeit focused more on state-mandated tests), these assessments will provide invaluable information on how students are progressing individually and collectively toward the district's expectations. For example, suppose a district set a goal to improve the amount of independent reading done by students across the grades. Data from random samples of students' reading logs could be analyzed to provide year-to-year comparisons of the amount (and perhaps type) of reading, to demonstrate progress (or lack of it) toward a stated goal. At the same time, individual student reading logs could be analyzed to determine the amount and kind of independent reading, as well as to use for instructional purposes.

Analyzing data brings us right back to the start of this framework, in that it informs the attributes themselves. Suppose our data show us that students' speaking and listening abilities make little contribution to state test performance, but they are occupying significant amounts of time and energy across the grades. This might lead us to emphasize these less while increasing time and energy to other aspects. Or we might conclude that although they aren't helping with test scores, they are contributing toward literacy in the workplace, where spoken interaction is critical. By continually forcing conversations about the various elements of the framework, the school district can adjust to changing literacy expectations from the state, the workplace, higher education, and society, as well as accommodate shifts in the student population. Gathering and analyzing data can bring clarity and focus to these conversations.

Summary

In summary, this language arts framework provides a consistent set of expectations for literacy from pre-K through grade 12 that supports the acquisition of critical language competencies within and beyond school. It also does the following:

First, it covers all six language arts areas (reading, writing, speaking, listening, viewing, and representing), as well as background knowledge—a critical contributor to literacy development.

Second, it emphasizes the few, essential expectations within each language arts area, as opposed to listing hundreds of detailed skills. This not only provides clarity of expectations; it also allows a district to meet not only the demands of school literacy (especially state examinations) but also the broader aspirations of literacy beyond school.

Third, it connects all aspects of language arts, from the attributes to instructional contributions to assessment and reporting. Analyzing the assessment data informs both instruction and professional development.

Fourth, it changes the way we think about the language arts curriculum, from a set of skills to be taught and mastered at each grade level to an approach in which all grade levels focus on the same literacy expectations, but with age- and grade-appropriate materials and experiences in each classroom.

Fifth, it changes the focus of the language arts curriculum toward what the teacher can do to nurture each student's growth toward the attributes rather than simply teach and assess a grade-level language arts curriculum. This does not imply an individualized curriculum for each child (most of the needed instruction and experiences can be common to all students) but rather a differentiated curriculum, in which the needs of individual children of varying abilities and experiences are met both in small and large group activities, as well as in one-to-one interactions.

Finally, it changes the definition of *consistency* in language arts from simply a set of shared curriculum materials to a set of shared literacy expectations. In fact, it goes further by articulating a small number of non-negotiable instructional contributions that allow considerable flexibility in the specific teaching and learning experiences in classrooms, yet provide consistency of best practice within and across grade levels.

2

LITERACY ATTRIBUTES

There is general consensus that schools should have expectations for what students should know, be able to do, or have experienced in language arts. Agreeing on what those expectations should be and how to articulate them, however, is another matter. And few schools clearly articulate their expectations.

This chapter is all about literacy expectations, or literacy *attributes*, as I prefer to call them. First, I'll define what I mean by *literacy attribute* and share literacy attributes from several projects I've undertaken with school districts. Next, I'll describe a number of sources for literacy expectations and why schools need to take them into consideration as they articulate their own. If this chapter inspires you to articulate your literacy expectations, what I have learned through trial and error with school colleagues might be useful as you travel a similar path. You'll find a description of the process I use with districts in Chapter Seven.

What Is a Literacy Attribute?

Attributes, as I said earlier, represent what we want a student to know, do, understand, and have experienced. *Knowing* includes knowing *what* (for example, background knowledge, knowledge of words, knowledge of written conventions) and knowing *how* (for example, how to figure out the meaning of an unknown word, the big idea of a book). *Doing* means sustained engagement in literacy behaviors (for example, reading on one's own, communicating through various media). *Understanding* includes making sense of informational and literary texts, grappling with big ideas, "interrogating" the text, and so on. *Having experienced* means the accumulated literacy and literary experiences that we expect students to have had across a significant time period (including ones they have brought with them and ones we have engaged them in—and especially those we have engaged them in because they didn't experience them before).

An attribute represents an "outer-layer" behavior or practice—one that identifies the most central of the many behaviors that make up a literate student. Attributes are articulated in the seven components that comprise literacy: *reading* (making sense of what is read), *listening* (making sense of what is heard), *viewing* (making sense of what is observed), *knowledge of the world* (understanding the world around and beyond oneself), *writing* (expressing ideas in written form), *speaking* (expressing ideas in spoken form), and *representing* (expressing ideas in a variety of media).

How is an attribute different from an expectation, an objective, a goal, or a standard? The problem is that these terms are often used interchangeably, so some readers will assume an attribute is the same as an expectation or even a standard. The reason I have used the term *attribute* is to distinguish it from the others. For me, expectations and goals are much broader in scope than attributes. An objective is much smaller. And a standard represents the level of performance within an expectation. However, the term *standard* is often used to define an expectation. One of New York's standards is "the student will read, write, listen and speak for literary response and evaluation." The actual level of performance is defined in the scoring rubrics of the state assessments. Given the way that the New York learning standards are written, I think of them as more akin to attributes than standards.

The term *attribute* is, for me, a more precise term to describe what a student looks like as a language user, in other words, what attributes the student possesses. It isn't just what he knows or can do but what he has experienced, and what he practices in daily life. But the term itself is not the issue; rather, it's what the term describes. So if my description of an attribute is the same as your definition of an expectation or standard, then feel free to use those terms!

A literacy attribute can serve two purposes. It can simply refer to characteristics of literate human beings in the seven components discussed earlier. But it can also be used to define characteristics we wish or expect students to have at any particular stage of their schooling. In other words, literacy attributes can simply describe what a language user looks like, or they can be used to describe what we want one to look like.

Another defining characteristic of attributes is that they don't try to articulate *all* the behaviors that make up literacy behaviors—just the most important ones. This doesn't negate the smaller behaviors, knowledge, and skills; rather, it places them within and underneath the attributes. In this way, we don't end up with long lists of literacy skills that fail to distinguish the parts from the whole.

You can see that attributes include much more than literacy skills. They are also not confined to single grades. I think literacy expectations should be couched in terms of *outcomes*, that is, expectations for students at the end of a significant period of formal schooling. I prefer twelfth grade; others suggest important milestones along the way (for example, fourth, eighth, and twelfth). On the one hand, these allow us to focus on the larger aims of schooling, keeping our eye on the bigger picture—something that listing small yearly goals fails to do. On the other hand, if we set out expectations that are too closely tied to the literacy expectations of a graduating high school student, our colleagues in preschool and the early primary grades will rightly complain that they cannot relate many of these expectations to their students.

The key to solving this lies in articulating the few, really critical, expectations and then making sure that they relate as well to a preschooler as to a senior in high school. When I first started working with schools, I wasn't able to figure out how to make this work with a single set of attributes that covered K–12. In recent years,

I've discovered that not only can it be done K–12, it also can be accomplished from birth through high school.

Does this mean that we shouldn't articulate literacy skills by grade level? Or by ages? Not at all. It suggests that these skills should be thought of as contributions to literacy attributes, as opposed to the attributes themselves. This will become much clearer in the chapter on instructional contributions.

Examples of Literacy Attributes

Now for some examples. My first attempt at helping a school articulate literacy attributes was in Manchester Elementary School, Vermont, in 1987. The charge to our language arts committee was to specify what we wanted a graduating eighth-grader to look like as a reader. I do recall it took a very long time, so I'm relieved that we only focused on reading, but eventually we came up with the following attributes for what we called the independent reader:

- Enjoys reading and reads for pleasure
- Has an extensive knowledge of the meanings of words
- Has a good understanding of what he/she reads, and can communicate this understanding in spoken or written form
- Responds to literature subjectively and analytically
- Reads widely and deeply
- Reads to obtain information
- Reads aloud fluently, confidently, and publicly
- Is confident, comfortable, self-assured, and independent as a reader

Since that time, I have worked with a number of school districts, and more recent lists of attributes include the full range of language arts components. Here is a sample list of attributes, compiled from several recent projects:

Reading

- Decodes/Reads fluently (applies appropriate reading strategies, knows conventions of print, identifies letters and letter sounds, knows sight words)
- Understands what is read (understands informational and literary text, understands big ideas, has an extensive reading vocabulary, applies effective comprehension strategies)
- Reads expressively
- Reads widely

Listening

- Is a critical and responsive listener

Viewing

- Is a critical and responsive viewer

Knowledge of the World

- Understands the world around and beyond himself/herself

Writing

- Communicates ideas effectively
- Organizes and fully develops writing
- Uses effective language/style
- Uses correct/appropriate mechanics (spelling, grammar, punctuation/capitalization, presentation/handwriting)

Speaking

- Communicates ideas effectively
- Uses appropriate techniques

Representing

- Communicates ideas effectively
- Uses appropriate media and techniques

These lists of literacy attributes are intended to capture, for a school district, what it considers to be the *most important* expectations for students as language users. The attributes are deliberately written in *clear, simple* English.

You can see from these examples that right from the first project, certain attributes emerged as critical ones, even though their wording varies. "Reading widely" is one of them, "decodes fluently" or "reads fluently" is another, and "understanding 'big ideas'" (or "reading deeply") is a third. Some attributes make it into some district's lists but not others. "Reads expressively" is one that some districts raise to the level of an attribute, while others tuck it inside other attributes or don't consider it critical enough to raise it to the level of an attribute. In some districts, "decodes fluently/reads fluently" is considered important enough to stand as an attribute on its own; in others, it is folded inside reading comprehension so as not to treat it as a prerequisite. These variations stem from different literacy and instructional philosophies held by educators in the various districts where I've worked.

Notice also how few attributes there are. This wasn't easy to accomplish, but when you limit yourself to just a handful, you can be sure they will represent the few, most critical expectations. It also ensures what diplomats call a frank exchange of views!

I should briefly discuss the issue of differently worded attributes for different levels (expressed in terms of grade levels, or age levels, or even developmental levels). You can see from the earlier list that "decoding fluency," especially if defined in terms of beginning reading, is probably not an important literacy expectation beyond grade 2. At the same time, if we want to articulate literacy attributes for preschoolers, most of the reading and writing attributes probably don't apply or would have to be completely reinterpreted. Let me share a couple of examples of how we have resolved this dilemma, in an attempt to cover a very broad span of literacy expectations.

In a recent project to articulate literacy attributes for children, birth through three years, we defined the attributes as follows:

Listening

- Makes sense of what is heard

Viewing

- Makes sense of what is observed

Reading

- Makes sense of what is read

Knowledge of the World

- Understands the world around and beyond himself/herself

Speaking

- Expresses ideas in spoken form

Representing

- Expresses ideas in a variety of media

Writing

- Expresses ideas in written form

Each of these attributes, except reading and writing, applies to a newborn and a three-year-old equally well. Reading and writing, in the sense that we typically define them, do not become viable attributes until children are at least thirty months old, sometimes earlier but mostly later. Prior to that, viewing and representing adequately represent how very young children make sense of visual displays and express meanings through gesturing, role-playing, manipulating toys, and drawing.

At the other end of the continuum (twelfth grade), where attributes such as "decoding fluently" typically do not apply (except to students with continuing language difficulties), here is an example of a set of high school literacy attributes:

Reading

- Is a critical, responsive, and insightful reader
- Understands different kinds of texts
- Reads widely

Listening

- Is a critical, responsive, and insightful listener

Viewing

- Is a critical, responsive, and insightful viewer

Writing

- Communicates ideas effectively
- Uses effective language/style
- Uses conventions appropriately

Speaking

- Communicates ideas effectively
- Uses appropriate techniques

Sources for Literacy Attributes

How you define literacy attributes depends a great deal on the sources you use to help guide your selections. Some of these sources are obvious, even mandatory, whereas others are less transparent and often overlooked. I want to start with educational ideologies, because these profoundly affect how literacy is defined, yet rarely intrude on school conversations about literacy expectations. I'll then discuss sources that are more familiar to educators: professional, state, and federal standards related to literacy, commercial textbooks' scope and sequences, and the literacy expectations of educators and the local community.

Educational and Literacy Ideologies

At first blush, it might seem self-evident that language arts comprises mainly reading and writing, speaking and listening, and that while there might be differences of opinion about how to teach them, why would there be any disagreement about the purpose of teaching them? However, beneath every aspect of language arts, there are arguments about what they mean, about the purpose of teaching them, and about how they privilege or disadvantage individual students or whole groups of students. So if you look at literacy expectations through philosophical lenses, you'll find there are competing *educational ideologies* that represent different beliefs about the nature and purpose of education in general and of literacy in particular. There are some literacy ideologies that dominate our thinking in American schools and several that challenge them.

According to Kohlberg and Mayer, the dominant educational ideology is *cultural transmission*, whose aim is to transmit from one generation to the next the attitudes, skills, and knowledge deemed appropriate for succeeding generations to acquire (Kohlberg and Mayer 1972). Kohlberg and Mayer argue that cultural transmission has two branches. One is an "academic" branch that defines literacy in terms of a student's ability to read and understand both classical and modern literature and to be articulate and sophisticated in written and oral expression. The other is a "utilitarian" branch that defines literacy as a survival skill in a complex technological society. In a utilitarian perspective, students should have functional literacy that allows them to participate successfully in everyday life (on the job, primarily, but also at home and in leisure activities). I have suggested (Walmsley 1981; Walmsley 1991) a third branch, which I call literacy skills, which defines literacy in terms of mastering school-related literacy skills thought to be necessary for advancement into higher education, work, or leisure.

Differences among the three branches of cultural transmission manifest themselves in a variety of ways. For example, each branch differs in its definition of a good reader or writer. The *academic* branch stresses higher-level understanding of canonical literature, whereas the *utilitarian* branch stresses what's called workplace literacy—understanding of largely nonfiction texts (for example, manuals, reports) and reading that's mostly connected to the workplace. Unlike the academic and utilitarian branches, the *literacy skills* branch appears to be neutral with respect to knowledge or the kinds of texts understood or created. Rather, it focuses on the skills and strategies needed to gain access to and communicate ideas but is not as concerned with the knowledge itself. Knowledge is considered something one can access once the reading and writing skills have been sufficiently well developed. It is precisely this lack of attention to content knowledge that comes under attack by critics such as E. D. Hirsch (Hirsch 1996) and precisely the focused attention to reading skills and strategies that is the hallmark of No Child Left Behind.

In secondary school, the academic perspective drives English programs for college-bound students, whereas the literacy skills and utilitarian perspectives drive the literacy programs for general education students and vocational students, respectively. In elementary school, the literacy skills perspective predominates, although one can catch glimpses of an academic perspective in literature-based programs (Walmsley and Walp 1990) and more recently in what are called core-knowledge approaches (Hirsch 2006).

Although cultural transmission is the dominant educational ideology, there are other ideologies competing for attention as goals for elementary and secondary school literacy programs. These include *romantic, cognitive developmental,* and *critical literacy.* They have different assumptions about the nature and purpose of literacy, and they imply quite different expectations for students.

The *romantic* ideology, derived originally from the work of philosophers such as Rousseau, exemplified in A. S. Neil's Summerhill School (Neil 1960) and more recently in the Whole Language movement (Goodman 1986), stresses the development of an individual's autonomy, ownership of self, or identity (Spring 1975). It defines literacy in terms of reading and writing for enjoyment and as contributions to personal development. The goal for literacy is determined as much by the individual as by the teacher or school. Also the act of reading is seen primarily in terms of a reader's construction of meaning—meaning that resides more inside the reader's head than within the text itself. Similarly, in writing, the romantic ideology stresses students' ownership of topics they write about, especially writing "voice."

A *cognitive-developmental* ideology, derived mainly from the work of Piaget (Piaget 1952) and Kohlberg and Mayer (1972), stresses the intellectual growth that emerges from interactions between language users and texts. Critical components of a cognitive-developmental ideology include knowledge of content, as well as the increasingly sophisticated ways in which readers and writers can interact with knowledge. Although this might appear to have the same aims as the academic branch, its focus is primarily on the development of thinking rather than familiarity with classical or contemporary canonical literature. Intellectual development could just as easily be achieved through interacting with nonclassical or even other kinds of "text" (for example, newspapers and magazines, and the Internet), provided that they have what Peterson and Eeds call multiple layers of meaning (Peterson and Eeds 1990), which would make them suitable for promoting intellectual growth. The work of Moffett (Moffett and Wagner 1992) is a prime example of a cognitive-developmental ideology pressed into the service of the English/language arts curriculum.

A *critical literacy* or *emancipatory* ideology derives from the work of Paulo Freire (Freire 1970; Freire and Macedo 1987) and more recently from literacy scholars (Shannon 1989; Bourdieu and Passeron 1990; Gee 1996; Gallego and Hollingsworth 2000; Collins 2003). A critical literacy ideology stresses the sociopolitical nature of literacy and invites readers to "interrogate" the texts they read, so they can grapple with the social and political issues that lie beneath texts. While a literacy skills approach would read *Dick and Jane* stories in the basal reader solely to acquire and practice reading skills, a critical literacy approach would interrogate the over-representation of white middle-class stereotypes. Although most parents and children would watch the movie *Free Willy* as family entertainment, Patrick Shannon uses it to challenge assumptions about corporate America, even with a first-grade child (Shannon 1995). In a critical literacy perspective, a good reader is one who is both aware of the social and political issues in texts and engages them, not merely for reading comprehension skills or intellectual growth but to change the relationship between oppressed and oppressors (Freire 1970).

So why should we be concerned about educational ideologies as we consider literacy expectations for our students? First, they jolt us out of our cozy assumption that literacy is simply the acquisition of reading and writing skills. Even if we stayed within a cultural transmission ideology (which, by definition, is the most dominant in public schools), we'd have to think about a balance between academic, utilitarian, and literacy skills. The academic branch challenges us to include literary understanding and writing with style in our expectations; the utilitarian exhorts us to take nonfiction and everyday reading materials seriously. The literacy skills perspective doesn't really challenge us, as it already dominates literacy expectations, especially in elementary school, and, thanks to No Child Left Behind, is enjoying renewed emphasis in the early grades.

Almost by definition, the "countercultural" ideologies (cognitive-developmental, romantic, critical literacy) greatly disturb our thinking about literacy expectations and challenge us to consider quite different kinds of expectations for our students. Of the three, the cognitive-developmental is the easiest to assimilate into our expectations, because it emphasizes what so many national reports and studies (for example, Lee, Grigg et al. 2007) tell us is lacking in America's schools: what Rexford Brown calls thoughtful literacy (Brown 1993), what James Britton (Pradl 1982) calls reading deeply. In New York State, where I live and teach, the standard that seems to be least well achieved is "reads, writes, speaks, listens for critical analysis and evaluation"—a standard that most closely exemplifies a cognitive-developmental ideology.

The romantic ideology, vilified by conservatives because it is associated with whole language, reminds us that once out of school, readers are free to read what they choose, write what they want, and engage in multiple literacies. If one of our goals for school literacy is to develop life-long literacy habits, then we need to take seriously the philosophy that directly supports these habits. Unfortunately, the term *romantic* has become synonymous with letting children take charge of their language arts programs.

Critical literacy is the most unsettling, because it seeks to change the relationship between language users and the texts they either read or create that have profound implications for how we even define the term *literacy*, or even if we can think other than *multiple literacies*. One of the tensions I feel all the time as I travel between the university and public schools is that critical literacy seems to be the dominant ideology in graduate literacy programs but a marginal source of literacy expectations in grade schools. Karen, a student in one of my graduate classes, summed it up so well. Karen, a full-time second-grade teacher in our doctoral program, told me how painful it was to go back and forth between the university, where she fully engaged in critical literacy issues, and her second-graders, where she fully engaged in "regular" literacy skills.

She couldn't figure out how to make the two worlds come together. As you'll see later, this is precisely my dilemma, too.

There are schools that exemplify countercultural transmission ideologies, and you'd only need to spend time in a Montessori or Waldorf school to see specific ideologies in action (Walmsley and Walmsley 1996). And there are examples from the professional literature where a specific countercultural transmission ideology has flourished, even if briefly, in a public school setting (Ostrow 1995; Levy 1996). But the weight of cultural transmission is overwhelming, and we rarely get more than a glimpse of what things would be like if, say, a critical literacy ideology should become dominant.

So why bother? Because it's in the tension between cultural transmission and countercultural ideologies that we make genuine progress. It never occurred to me as a child, growing up in England with history books that proudly colored most of the world in colonial red, that there might be an alternate view of colonialism. When I first came to the United States, I remember being comforted by the fact that the literature studied by American high school students was, in large measure, the literature I had studied in school. But I also now remember with huge embarrassment how much I opposed the concept of mainstreaming children with special needs (in England, when I was growing up, these children weren't just absent from classrooms; they were absent from the schools altogether), and I even objected strongly to balancing gender references in articles and books. It is hard now to imagine how I could have opposed either of these in the first place. But I am sure I'm not alone. It might not have occurred to you, if you learned to read with Dick and Jane, that these seemingly innocent texts were perpetuating the subjugation of minorities. Even now, how aware are we that because of political pressures, the very language children are exposed to in their textbooks has been sanitized by both left- and right-wing censors (Ravitch 2003)? It is hard to imagine anything but a cultural transmission ideology as the dominant engine of public school literacy, but it is also difficult to see how a democracy can survive without the continuous barbs of countercultural ideologies. In fact, the tension between them is what defines literacy in a democratic society. And that is why literacy ideologies have to occupy significant space in any discussion about literacy expectations.

Finally, an important lesson to be gained from studying countercultural perspectives is that literacy has always been a vehicle that consciously and unconsciously privileges some literacies while disparaging others, which has long-lasting consequences for both the privileged and the disparaged. If literacy is to play its rightful part in the quest for social justice, then countercultural perspectives on literacy have to be included in school discussions about literacy expectations, not just in the universities.

Language Arts Standards

Another source for literacy attributes is language arts standards, which come from professional organizations such as the NCTE, the IRA, and the NAEYC or from the state departments of education. Let's start with the professional language arts standards. A few years ago, a joint task force of the NCTE and the IRA created a list of twelve standards (NCTE 1996):

1. Students read a wide range of print and non-print texts to build an understanding of texts, of themselves, and of the cultures of the United States and the world; to acquire new information; to respond to the needs and demands of society and the workplace; and for personal fulfillment. Among these texts are fiction and nonfiction, classic and contemporary works.

2. Students read a wide range of literature from many periods in many genres to build an understanding of the many dimensions (e.g., philosophical, ethical, aesthetic) of human experience.

3. Students apply a wide range of strategies to comprehend, interpret, evaluate, and appreciate texts. They draw on their prior experience, their interactions with other readers and writers, their knowledge of word meaning and of other texts,

their word identification strategies, and their understanding of textual features (e.g., sound-letter correspondence, sentence structure, context, graphics).

4. Students adjust their use of spoken, written, and visual language (e.g., conventions, style, vocabulary) to communicate effectively with a variety of audiences and for different purposes.

5. Students employ a wide range of strategies as they write and use different writing process elements appropriately to communicate with different audiences for a variety of purposes.

6. Students apply knowledge of language structure, language conventions (e.g., spelling and punctuation), media techniques, figurative language, and genre to create, critique, and discuss print and non-print texts.

7. Students conduct research on issues and interests by generating ideas and questions, and by posing problems. They gather, evaluate, and synthesize data from a variety of sources (e.g., print and non-print texts, artifacts, people) to communicate their discoveries in ways that suit their purpose and audience.

8. Students use a variety of technological and information resources (e.g., libraries, databases, computer networks, video) to gather and synthesize information and to create and communicate knowledge.

9. Students develop an understanding of and respect for diversity in language use, patterns, and dialects across cultures, ethnic groups, geographic regions, and social roles.

10. Students whose first language is not English make use of their first language to develop competency in the English language arts and to develop understanding of content across the curriculum.

11. Students participate as knowledgeable, reflective, creative, and critical members of a variety of literacy communities.

12. Students use spoken, written, and visual language to
accomplish their own purposes (e.g., for learning, enjoyment,
persuasion, and the exchange of information).

Given the earlier discussion about educational ideologies, it's
interesting to note how the two professional organizations that
have the most to do with literacy theory and pedagogy chose to
avoid any direct reference to critical literacy—just a hint of it in
Standard 11. But I think it's fair to say that these standards equita-
bly represent all the other literacy ideologies.

New York State's Language Arts Standards are as follows
(New York State Education Department 1996):

*Standard 1: Students will read, write, listen, and speak for information
and understanding.* As listeners and readers, students will collect data,
facts, and ideas; discover relationships, concepts, and generalizations;
and use knowledge generated from oral, written, and electronically
produced texts. As speakers and writers, they will use oral and written
language to acquire, interpret, apply, and transmit information.

*Standard 2: Students will read, write, listen, and speak for literary
response and expression.* Students will read and listen to oral, written,
and electronically produced texts and performances, relate texts and
performances to their own lives, and develop an understanding of
the diverse social, historical, and cultural dimensions the texts and
performances represent. As speakers and writers, students will use
oral and written language for self-expression and artistic creation.

*Standard 3: Students will read, write, listen, and speak for critical
analysis and evaluation.* As listeners and readers, students will analyze experiences, ideas, information, and issues presented by others using a variety of established criteria. As speakers and writers,
they will present, in oral and written language and from a variety of
perspectives, their opinions and judgments on experiences, ideas,
information and issues.

*Standard 4: Students will read, write, listen, and speak for social
interaction.* Students will use oral and written language for effective

social communication with a wide variety of people. As readers and listeners, they will use the social communications of others to enrich their understanding of people and their views.

Notice how these two sets of standards describe expectations largely in terms of literacy processes (that is, what students should be engaging in) rather than as outcomes (that is, what students should know or how well they should perform). In other states, the trend seems to be a combination of process and outcome expectations. For example, Louisiana State Language Arts Standards are as follows (Louisiana State Department of Education 2004):

1. Students read, comprehend, and respond to a range of materials, using a variety of strategies for different purposes.

2. Students write competently for a variety of purposes and audiences.

3. Students communicate using standard English grammar, usage, sentence structure, punctuation, capitalization, spelling, and handwriting.

4. Students demonstrate competence in speaking and listening as tools for learning and communicating.

5. Students locate, select, and synthesize information from a variety of texts, media, references, and technological sources to acquire and communicate knowledge.

6. Students read, analyze, and respond to literature as a record of life experiences.

7. Students apply reasoning and problem solving skills to reading, writing, speaking, listening, viewing, and visually representing.

Notice here how Louisiana's expectations are articulated primarily in terms of skills or strategies to be learned and demonstrated.

School districts cannot ignore their state's English/Language Arts Standards, so these need to be carefully analyzed and always included in discussions about articulating literacy expectations.

So why not simply use these state expectations as written? It's a good question.

I don't think that state standards should be the sole source, for several reasons. The first is that states do not always include all language arts components. In New York State, for example, there's no *viewing* or *representing* in the standards, despite being significant components of both literacy and content area assessments.

Second, if you look carefully at the NCTE/IRA standards, and compare them with those of your home state, you'll probably see some important goals in each that are not covered in the other. Having the perspective of literacy professionals from across the entire country is particularly important in articulating literacy expectations that the framers of a state document overlooked or deemed unimportant. For example, one of the NCTE/IRA standards (*Students participate as knowledgeable, reflective, creative, and critical members of a variety of literacy communities*) captures an important expectation that my state's standards don't really touch on, and even if it doesn't make it into a school district's expectations, it is worthy of consideration.

Third, I like to think that even though a state has a compelling and legitimate interest in articulating its educational standards, the local school district has its interests, too, and these should not be simply suppressed in favor of the state's. Although sometimes I wonder if there's any local autonomy left, education is still legally a community responsibility, so exercising this responsibility, with due attention and respect for state mandates, is an important obligation. There are always local conditions and contexts for literacy that necessitate additional or different literacy expectations, and districts do their students no favors by blindly accepting their state's literacy standards as their own.

Federal Standards

Traditionally, the federal government has used its bully pulpit to set ambitious goals for education, but they tend to be rather vague.

For example, in the Clinton administration, the Goals 2000 legislation included the following:

> By the year 2000, all students will leave grades 4, 8, and 12 having demonstrated competency over challenging subject matter including English, mathematics, science, foreign languages, civics and government, economics, arts, history, and geography, and every school in America will ensure that all students learn to use their minds well, so they may be prepared for responsible citizenship, further learning, and productive employment in our Nation's modern economy.

In the Bush administration's No Child Left Behind legislation, literacy expectations are framed in terms of both areas and performance criteria (for example, reading on grade level at third grade; satisfactory annual progress on a scientifically reliable and valid reading assessments). For early reading, No Child Left Behind lays out specific literacy components it expects students to be explicitly taught and assessed:

- *Phonemic awareness*: the ability to hear and identify sounds in spoken words.
- *Phonics*: the relationship between the letters of written language and the sounds of spoken language.
- *Fluency*: the capacity to read text accurately and quickly.
- *Vocabulary*: the words students must know to communicate effectively.
- *Comprehension*: the ability to understand and gain meaning from what has been read.

Although these areas of literacy and the criteria for assessment are much more specifically defined than in any earlier federal legislation, NCLB really doesn't articulate comprehensive goals for literacy as a whole. It barely mentions listening, speaking, or even writing. Its definition of comprehension is quite literal, and it excludes literary understanding. Admittedly, NCLB was never intended to be comprehensive in its scope or expectations; rather, its major thrust is to ensure that specific goals for early reading instruction are carried out in every public school in the nation.

Nonetheless, given the high-stakes testing, as well as the fiscal and political consequences of failing to meet NCLB's requirements for annual yearly progress, a district would be foolhardy not to include its expectations in discussions about its own literacy expectations. However, given NCLB's narrow focus, making it the primary source for literacy expectations would be equally foolhardy. Nevertheless, I suspect that many schools are doing just that, especially when their annual yearly progress falls far short of expectations.

Scope-and-Sequence Charts

One of the most common sources for literacy expectations in a school district is the scope-and-sequence charts. These are mostly borrowed from commercial basal reading series, but they also come from textbooks and state education departments. I can see the appeal. Everything is laid out by grade level; it's neat and tidy, and the work has already been done by someone else.

For example, if your district had access to, or already used, the *Harcourt Brace Trophy Series*, you'd find in the teacher's manual an eight-page chart, detailing for each grade, K–6, hundreds of literacy skills, organized under the major categories of reading, writing, listening, and speaking. Each category is further broken down into subcategories (for example, reading breaks down into eighteen subcategories ranging from phonemic awareness to literary responses and analysis), then each subcategory is further subdivided (for example, reading comprehension is broken down into forty-one sub-subcategories, such as organizing information in alphabetical order, sequence, and summarize). For each subskill, the grade at which it is tested and taught is identified.

Some states also break down their standards into grade-level expectations. I shared the Louisiana English/Language Arts Standards earlier. In a forty-nine-page document that accompanies the standards, it lists specific skills at each grade level. Here are the expectations for Standard 1 (Reading) at sixth grade:

Sixth Grade
Reading and Responding
Standard 1:

1. Identify word meanings using a variety of strategies, including:
   - using context clues (e.g., definition, restatement, example, contrast)
   - using structural analysis (e.g., roots, affixes)
   - determining word origins (etymology)
   - using knowledge of idioms
   - explaining word analogies (ELA-1-M1)

2. Identify common abbreviations, symbols, acronyms, and multiple-meaning words (ELA-1-M1)

3. Develop specific vocabulary (e.g., scientific, content-specific, current events) for various purposes (ELA-1-M1)

4. Identify and explain story elements, including:
   - theme development
   - character development
   - relationship of word choice and mood
   - plot sequence (e.g., exposition, rising action, climax, falling action, resolution) (ELA-1-M2)

5. Identify and explain literary and sound devices, including:
   - foreshadowing
   - flashback
   - imagery
   - onomatopoeia (ELA-1-M2)

6. Answer literal and inferential questions in oral and written responses about ideas and information in grade-appropriate texts, including:

- comic strips
- editorial cartoons
- speeches (ELA-1-M3)

7. Explain the connections between ideas and information in a variety of texts (e.g., journals, technical specifications, advertisements) and real-life situations and other texts (ELA-1-M4)

Standard 6:

8. Compare and contrast cultural characteristics (e.g., customs, traditions, viewpoints) found in national, world, and multicultural literature (ELA-6-M1)

9. Compare and contrast elements (e.g., plot, setting, characters, theme) in a variety of genres (ELA-6-M2)

10. Use knowledge of the distinctive characteristics to classify and interpret elements of various genres, including:

- fiction (e.g., myths, historical fiction)
- nonfiction (e.g., newspaper articles, magazine articles)
- poetry (e.g., lyric, narrative)
- drama (e.g., short plays) (ELA-6-M3)

Standard 7:

11. Demonstrate understanding of information in grade-appropriate texts using a variety of strategies, including:

- sequencing events and steps in a process
- summarizing and paraphrasing information
- identifying stated or implied main ideas and supporting details
- comparing and contrasting literary elements and ideas
- making simple inferences and drawing conclusions

- predicting the outcome of a story or situation
- identifying literary devices (ELA-7-M1)

12. Examine and explain the relationship between life experiences and texts to generate solutions to problems (ELA-7-M2)

13. Use technical information and other available resources (e.g., software programs, manuals) to solve problems (ELA-7-M2)

14. Analyze an author's stated or implied purpose for writing (e.g., to explain, to entertain, to persuade, to inform, to express personal attitudes or beliefs) (ELA-7-M3)

15. Identify persuasive techniques (e.g., unsupported inferences, faulty reasoning, generalizations) that reflect an author's viewpoint (perspective) in texts (ELA-7-M3)

16. Analyze grade-appropriate print and nonprint texts using various reasoning skills, including:
    - identifying cause-effect relationships
    - raising questions
    - reasoning inductively and deductively
    - generating a theory or hypothesis
    - skimming/scanning
    - distinguishing facts from opinions and probability (ELA-7-M4)

Although these scope-and-sequence charts give the appearance of including everything a school or district would need in terms of literacy expectations, they have some serious shortcomings, some of which I have discussed earlier.

First, they almost always define literacy in terms of the acquisition of discrete literacy skills. In most cases, these lists are simply modern versions of the subskills lists produced by researchers at the end of the World War II, based on factor analyses of scores on reading achievement tests. True, several aspects of early reading have been added, such as concepts of print (knowing left-to-right and top-to-bottom directionality and identifying front and back cover of a book), and phonemic awareness. These lists essentially define literacy expectations as mastery of literally hundreds of discrete literacy subskills.

Second, scope-and-sequence charts say little about the relationship between mastery of subskills and outcomes such as reading fluently or understanding what is read. What is the relationship between the acquisition of these skills and, say, one of the NCTE/IRA standards: *Students participate as knowledgeable, reflective, creative, and critical members of a variety of literacy communities?* Will students automatically participate in these literacy communities as a direct consequence of mastering the subskills? If so, how? And where is the evidence that they do?

Third, these lists generally ignore anything that isn't a discrete skill. For example, shouldn't we have "reading widely" as an expectation, not just in terms of an activity in school but also as a goal for the language arts program itself?

Finally, I worry about the sheer number of skills listed. My experience is that these binders of skills sit on shelves; they are simply too thick and full of details to be practical guides to daily classroom instruction. The fatter the binder, the higher the probability it will gather dust. And the more these lists are used to guide instruction, the more likely that important aspects of literacy, such as wide and deep reading, will be neglected.

Looked at from the perspective of literacy ideologies, these scope-and sequence charts exemplify the literacy skills branch of cultural transmission, almost to a tee. Our expectation for students is "knowing" the literacy skills. What they do with these skills, however, apparently isn't relevant to our literacy mission.

My concern about scope-and-sequence lists is not that they have no place in the language arts curriculum or classroom; rather, that they should not be the primary source for literacy expectations. Almost all of them, especially the smaller ones, are instructional contributions. Expectations should list what we want as outcomes of instructional contributions, not the instruction itself. As I write this, I'm aware that there's a fine line between what we want students to know or do as a consequence of what we teach them or engage them in, and what we want them to know or do within the instruction itself. This should become clearer as I explain how attributes differ from instructional contributions.

Collective Judgment of School and Community Members

I've left this source until the last, but it's not the least important. In fact, this source is both one of the most important and one of the most neglected. It is true that school and community members are often the source for one set of expectations—a district's mission statement. This might sour one to the idea of drawing on school and community members for literacy expectations. Mission statements crafted largely by lay people often end up as verbose, overly platitudinous, and frequently ungrammatical statements that are hard to translate into meaningful expectations:

> As a central school district rich in heritage, diversity, and pride, faced with the needs of an ever-changing community, the mission of this central school district is to create for all students a productive!, challenging!, and safe! Educational environment in which they can acquire civic values and learning skills necessary to be successful; this will be provided through a dynamic partnership among the students, schools, and community working together toward specific, clearly defined expectations.

I don't place too much credence in mission statements and wonder if their purpose is largely ceremonial and hortatory. But I've learned a lot from studying them. It's very hard to articulate worthwhile goals or expectations in clear, simple, language. It's also hard to write anything with a large group of people. And yet, done right, a mission statement can communicate clearly what we expect of our students and of ourselves. Having seen it done right, even occasionally, has given me hope that literacy expectations can follow a similar path:

The program is designed to develop students' confidence in themselves as learners, to instill a love of learning and a desire to learn, and to enable students to develop the knowledge, skills, and attitudes needed to communicate effectively, understand the world around them, and participate effectively in a democratic society.

Later in the book (see Chapter Nine), I'll describe in detail techniques I have been using and am still developing to capture the literacy expectations of local educators and community members. Here let me just reiterate the importance of including them as a legitimate source for expectations and suggest that if done in the right way—working toward articulating the fewest, most critical, expectations, as opposed to everything, including the kitchen sink—this is a viable exercise and a much-needed one. As school districts set out to articulate what they want their students to look like as language users, they frequently ignore the fact that teachers, parents, and community members already have a pretty clear idea of what they expect.

For example, if you were to tell me that your friend Dmitri was a good reader, and I knew his age to be eleven, I think I'd have a pretty good idea what you meant. I'd conjure up a picture of a third-grader who read fluently and had a good understanding of material he read. If Dmitri were an adult, you probably wouldn't describe him as a good reader, unless it was in contrast to some other characteristics, such as, he was not a native English speaker. We constantly use terms like *good reader*, *writes well*, *good listener*, *excellent speaker* to describe people's language abilities, and when we do so, we generally aren't quizzed about the precise meanings. In the social context of conversation, these "attributes" are fairly well understood. And we make allowances in our understanding of them to take account of the age of the person being described. So we calibrate a phrase like "she writes so well," depending on whether it's a first-grader or an accomplished novelist we're talking about. Interestingly enough, when we use these terms, we are more likely to be emphasizing meaning over mechanics. When someone is described as a good listener, it's not likely that the person's hearing acuity is being remarked on but her ability to understand what she hears and, especially in the case of a good listener, the empathy she offers the speaker and her engagement in the conversation.

The reason I share these examples is because in the real world, we have some common understandings about what we think an accomplished user of the language looks like. In other words, we not only have a pretty good idea about what being literate is; we already have many of the descriptors in place.

However, when schools try to articulate literacy expectations, they all too frequently step out of their "ordinary person" role and into the jargon and technical language of literacy educators and scope-and-sequence charts. And they often forget that the way they define literacy beyond the school playground needs to be taken into consideration when defining it inside the classroom, both in terms of what counts as literacy and the words used to describe it. Tapping into these personal, school, and community expectations is as important as drawing on state or professional standards.

Summary

What started as a seemingly simple exercise in 1987 to articulate what a K–8 school in Vermont wanted a graduating eighth-grader to look like as a reader has, twenty years later, ended up as a full-fledged articulation of what we want a student to look like as a reader, writer, listener, speaker, and representer from birth through grade 12. It hasn't been a simple exercise, and it's still ongoing, but the original idea of being able to state in clear, ordinary language what's most important in terms of expectations for literacy has, for the most part, been accomplished in the districts I have worked with.

There will always be competing definitions of what counts as "fully literate," as well as what a district's literacy expectations should include and what terms should be used to describe these, but what this framework demonstrates is that it is possible to articulate the few, most important literacy expectations and to do so across a wide span (birth through grade 12).

3

INSTRUCTIONAL CONTRIBUTIONS

I have titled this chapter "Instructional Contributions" rather than "The Language Arts Curriculum" or "Teaching Language Arts" because I want to propose a shift in emphasis in how we think about language arts instruction. Instead of just teaching language arts, devoting this or that amount of time to various components (for example, reading skills, comprehension, composing, or spelling), I suggest that language arts instruction should have literacy attributes as its primary focus. In other words, everything that goes on in a language arts classroom has an overarching goal, namely to contribute to each student's literacy attributes. It makes sense, then, to use the term *instructional contributions*. They are what teachers and specialists provide to ensure that students make the best possible progress toward the attributes. Saying that your first-grade classrooms use Scott, Foresman's *Reading Street* Series doesn't convey the same goal for language arts.

Instructional contributions include *direct and indirect instruction* (for example, teaching comprehension skills explicitly or incidentally through guided reading) and *literacy experiences* (for example, independent reading and writing, listening to read-alouds). Instructional contributions also encompass everything that teachers do to motivate students to learn, what they do to engage students' parents, and what materials—commercial or homegrown—they use in their classrooms. Of course, there are instructional contributions offered by others outside school by parents, relatives, friends, television, radio, the Internet, museums, and libraries, to name just a few. These are not trivial contributions (sometimes I wonder if children learn more outside of school than inside it, especially on the school bus), but they aren't the primary focus of this chapter.

In this chapter, I'll start by defining what I mean by *instructional contributions* and share examples of them. But first, I need to distinguish between two kinds of instructional contributions: *non-negotiables* and *instructional activities*. *Non-negotiable contributions* represent instruction and experiences that every teacher and specialist must provide all students. The idea is that when each educator implements these non-negotiables, all students will make the best possible progress toward the attributes. To ensure that the non-negotiables are implemented, teachers also need to provide appropriate *instructional activities*.[1] These instructional activities represent the accommodations needed to address the particular strengths and needs of diverse students, as well as put to good use the craft and expertise of individual teachers. Instructional activities also represent legitimately different instructional methods and materials to achieve common goals.

Next, I'll describe various language arts containers (in other words, the ways in which language arts instruction is organized and actually delivered in classrooms) and discuss how they can best be used to nurture students' progress toward the attributes.

Finally, I want to address the issue of how a district might ensure that the non-negotiables are actually non-negotiable.

---

[1]Until recently, I used the term *negotiable contributions* to define these instructional activities. The idea was that there are non-negotiables that must be done, and then negotiables that represent a variety of ways in which the non-negotiables can be met. This has turned out to be confusing to educators, who think that there are non-negotiables that they have to do, and negotiables that they can do, not realizing that the negotiables are directly linked to the non-negotiables. By using the term *instructional activities*—first suggested to me by my colleague Lynnette Pannucci—the relationship between what must be done, and the various instructional activities that support them, becomes much clearer.

Non-Negotiable Instructional Contributions

When I first started working on the framework in the late 1980s, I thought in terms of literacy activities that would best promote growth toward the attributes. But it wasn't long before I realized that school districts weren't too happy about the idea of just recommending instructional activities, in hopes that teachers would use them. So the idea of articulating "must-do" or non-negotiable instructional contributions came into being. However, I clung onto the notion that there had to be flexibility to accommodate the diversity of students' needs and to recognize teachers' strengths and interests, so the notion of appropriate—and differentiated—instructional activities followed on the heels of the non-negotiables.

Let me first share a set of non-negotiable contributions. (Later, in Chapter Nine, I'll describe the process I typically use in order to arrive at them in consultation with educators). Here is a complete set of non-negotiables for reading, which in one district comprised the following two reading attributes (note there are only two reading attributes, but several subattributes are tucked inside them):

- *Understands What Is Read* (decodes fluently, reads expressively, understands informational text, understands literary texts, understands "big ideas," has an extensive reading vocabulary)
- *Reads Widely*

In the description that follows, I'll give a brief definition of the subattribute and follow that with the non-negotiables.

Decodes Fluently

By *decoding fluently* we mean that a student is able to decode continuous text at an appropriate level, using appropriate reading strategies, at an appropriate rate, and with accuracy. This includes understanding basic conventions of print (for example, that text flows from top to bottom, left to right; what simple punctuation marks are; one-to-one correspondence between text and oral reading); recognizing letters of the alphabet and knowing their sounds; demonstrating phonemic awareness (awareness of the alphabetic basis for the language; the ability to hear, identify, and manipulate sounds in spoken words); recognizing sight words (high-frequency words that a reader instantly recognizes without having to sound them out).

We expect that *decoding fluency* will be attained by all students by the end of second grade. This attribute would only apply to students beyond second grade, if they had not yet attained decoding fluency, that is, had not yet reached Level 28 on the DRA (Beaver and Carter 2006).

Non-Negotiable Instructional Contributions
to Decoding Fluency:

- Provide a print-rich environment.
- Model, teach, and practice strategies for using/integrating cueing systems (visual, meaning, structure) in authentic, continuous text.
- Model, teach, and have students practice basic conventions of print (for example, left-to-right progression, return sweep, one-to-one correspondence).
- Model, teach, and have students practice decoding skills through daily reading and writing experiences.
- Provide appropriate direct instruction in decoding skills when necessary.

Reads Expressively

Reading expressively is a valuable skill, both in school (for example, being able to read aloud to peers or a wider audience) and beyond (for example, reading to one's family). Reading expressively both contributes to reading comprehension and provides evidence of understanding. (Although I recognize that reading expressively might more accurately be categorized as an expressive rather than receptive literacy attribute, we felt that it belonged with other reading attributes.)

*Non-Negotiable Instructional Contributions
to Reading Expressively:*

- Provide regular opportunities for students to read aloud (one-on-one, small group, large group).
- Model, teach, and have students practice strategies for reading with expression (for example, audibility, phrasing, intonation).

Understands Informational Texts

Traditionally, schools have emphasized fiction over nonfiction in their reading material, and this attribute aims to better balance the two. Reading across the curriculum demands proficiency in informational reading (for example, textbooks, primary source documents, nonfiction trade books, magazines), as does the increasing amount and complexity of informational text beyond school. Further, New York State standards emphasize the importance of a thorough rather than a literal understanding of text.

*Non-Negotiable Instructional Contributions to
Understanding Informational Texts:*

- Engage students in reading a wide range of informational texts (both print and electronic media), representing a variety of content and voices.
- Model, teach, and have students practice and reflect on strategies for reading and understanding informational text (for example, self-monitoring, making connections, active questioning, accessing text features).
- Model, teach, and have students practice supporting responses to informational text with appropriate evidence.

Understands Literary Texts

Literary texts include classic and contemporary literature in both prose and poetic forms. New York State standards emphasize students' understanding of *literary aspects* of a book or other material (for example, the way a character is portrayed, the writer's style, the organization or development of a story, literary elements) and the students' *personal responses* to the work.

*Non-Negotiable Instructional Contributions
to Understanding Literary Texts:*

- Provide frequent opportunities for students to read, respond, and discuss diverse forms of literature.
- Expose students to and teach a wide variety of literary styles, elements, and techniques.
- Model, teach, and have students practice supporting literary or personal responses with appropriate evidence.

Understands "Big Ideas"

The term *big ideas,* in both informational and literary texts, refers not just to main ideas of sentences or paragraphs but underlying themes. New York State standards emphasize reading for *critical analysis and evaluation,* stressing the importance of students' ability to analyze, synthesize, relate, critique, and evaluate big ideas.

*Non-Negotiable Instructional Contributions to
Understanding Big Ideas:*

- Engage students in many and varied texts with multiple layers of meaning (in read-alouds, guided/shared, and independent reading).
- Provide opportunities for students to revise and deepen their understanding of texts through discussion and reflection.

- Model, teach, and have students practice and reflect on a range of strategies for analyzing, making connections, and synthesizing multiple layers of meaning.

Has an Extensive Reading Vocabulary

We want our students to have good reading vocabularies—to know the words that readers encounter in the books and other material and know what they mean. There are several kinds of reading vocabularies: common words that have multiple meanings depending on the context (for example, *run a mile*, *run a business*), words that are primarily technical (for example, *soffit*, *line-item veto*), words that are primarily figurative (for example, *parenthetically*), and so on.

Non-Negotiable Instructional Contributions
to Reading Vocabulary:

- Expose students to rich vocabulary in a wide variety of literature (through read-alouds, shared reading, independent reading), and draw students' attention to vocabulary in these contexts.
- Model, teach, and analyze multiple meanings of words, figurative language, technical language, content area vocabulary, and the importance of rich vocabulary.
- Engage in conversation that will enrich students' vocabulary.
- Model, teach, and practice strategies for figuring out meanings of words (for example, context clues, root words, affixes)

Reads Widely

Reading widely is a critical ingredient of reading well. By this, we mean two things: first, that students have read a substantial number of books and other material *on their own*; second, that they have read across literary genres (fiction, nonfiction, poetry), different forms of print (books, magazines, newspapers, primary source documents), different purposes (information, pleasure), diversity (of culture, authors, gender), and from a variety of content areas (for example, science, social studies, music, art).

Non-Negotiable Instructional Contributions
to Reading Widely:

- Model reading from a variety of printed sources (*genre*—fiction, nonfiction, poetry, content areas; *diversity*—author, culture, gender, topics; *forms of print*—books, magazines, newspapers, documents, electronic media; *purpose*—information, pleasure).
- Make available a substantial amount and a wide variety of printed and electronic material (in classroom, school library).
- Provide frequent (daily, in elementary school) opportunities and encouragement for students to read a substantial amount and to read widely (including self-selected, teacher-prompted material).
- Provide frequent opportunities for students to share reading experiences.

Guidelines for Articulating Non-negotiable Contributions. As you read the non-negotiables, you may have found yourself saying, "So, what's new? I do all these things anyway." If you did, you aren't alone, and I take your reaction as a compliment. However, getting to this point isn't as easy as you might think.

In my projects with schools, I have developed the following guidelines for articulating non-negotiables:

- The goal is to articulate the *fewest* number of critical instructional contributions.
- Non-negotiables need to apply to the widest range of grades and literacy levels (there are exceptions to this, which I'll discuss later).

- Each non-negotiable contribution has to focus specifically on the attribute (yes, having a good breakfast is important, but what is its unique contribution to understanding big ideas?).
- Non-negotiables don't specify particular instructional activities, because there is never a single teaching strategy or literacy experience that applies in every situation and therefore *has* to be used by every teacher.

Benefits of Articulating Non-negotiables. Narrowing down the possible non-negotiables to the few critical ones is a difficult and harrowing process, but the exercise itself has benefits that extend well beyond itself. One thing it does is help teachers sort out in their own minds what's really important to focus on in the limited time they all have for literacy instruction. I sometimes think that there's such an emphasis placed on creating activities in classrooms that teachers often lose sight of their purpose. Having to articulate a direct connection between a literacy attribute and the major instructional activities necessary to help students acquire it is quite an eye-opener. It shows how much that is done in classrooms really falls short of intentional, purposeful teaching.

Another benefit of this exercise is that although almost everyone agrees on contributions like providing time for students to read independently, most also agree that this time is frequently invaded by other activities to a point where it isn't regular or it's something that's done after other priorities have been taken care of. Once a contribution becomes non-negotiable, then it has to be included in the language arts program and cannot be invaded by other activities.

Finally, there's a sense of relief that comes from finalizing the non-negotiables, because they provide teachers with a finite set of contributions that cover what needs to be done, without over-prescribing the specifics.

You can again see why getting the literacy attributes right has profound consequences. If we are to insist that teachers implement the non-negotiables, then they need to be drawn from literacy attributes we really want our students to acquire.

Sources for Non-negotiables. In articulating non-negotiable instructional contributions, I encourage school districts to draw on a number of sources. I've already alluded to the collective wisdom and experience of literacy teachers and specialists in the district. They are a primary source. However, there are other useful sources to draw on.

I've found that state education documents are very helpful. For example, New York State's English/Language Arts Standards include extensive listings of activities that support each of the standards. The downside of documents such as these is that they tend to fuel teachers' proclivity for making their own extensive lists of instructional activities, which in turn defeats the whole purpose of articulating the few, really important non-negotiables. Such lists are in fact better for creating instructional activities to implement non-negotiables than for articulating the non-negotiables themselves.

Another source is the professional literature, especially books and articles that focus broadly on literacy across elementary, middle, and high school—for example, Allington and Cunningham's *Schools That Work* (Allington and Cunningham 1996); Harwayne's *Lifetime Guarantees* (Harwayne 2000); Allington's *What Really Matters for Struggling Readers* (Allington 2006); Hirsch's *The Schools We Need* (Hirsch 1996); Cooper's *Literacy: Helping Children Construct Meaning* (Cooper and Kiger 2006); Myers's *Changing Our Minds* (Myers 1996); Langer's *Envisioning Literature* (Langer 1995).

An essential resource for non-negotiables is the research literature. Particularly useful are the handbooks of research: *The Handbook of Research on Teaching English Language Arts* (Flood 2002); *The Handbook of Reading Research* (Kamil 2000). I would also include the National Research Council's *Preventing Reading Difficulties in Young Children* (Snow, Burns et al. 1998) and the National Reading Panel's *Teaching Children to Read* (National Institute of Child Health and Human Development 2000). Further, research journals in the literacy field, such as *Reading Research Quarterly*, the *Journal* of Reading, the Journal of Adolescent and Adult Literacy, the Journal of Literacy Research, Language Arts, and Research in the Teaching of English present the latest findings of research in literacy. Journals that cover broader topics in education, such as Curriculum Inquiry, Educational Leadership, and Elementary School Journal, also publish relevant articles on literacy pedagogy from time to time.

What these books, articles, and reports contribute to our discussion of appropriate non-negotiables are the fruits of ongoing research and pedagogy in the teaching of literacy. On some issues, there seems to be unanimous agreement—for example, the need for teachers to model literacy strategies for their students. In some areas, there are sharp disagreements. For example, the National Reading Panel casts serious doubt on the efficacy of having students engage in independent, free-choice reading, saying that the research doesn't support it. However, research findings presented by Allington (Allington 2006) and Krashen (Krashen 2004) strongly support independent reading. (In fact, I recently attended a workshop presented by Reading First, and I was quite surprised to find the speaker strongly advocating independent reading as a critical aspect of an effective reading program, based strictly on the research findings of the National Reading Panel.)

Including research and professional literature that presents a wide range of viewpoints is an essential component of the process of reaching out to sources for non-negotiable contributions. At the same time, a district will have to make up its own mind about which path to take where there are conflicts in the literature. It should do so only *after* considering the alternatives, not before.

One Set of Non-negotiables or Many? Inevitably, the question will arise: Should there be a single set of non-negotiables, covering, say, pre-K through grade 12, or should there be several? In some districts, we have created non-negotiables that are intentionally designed to cover the entire span. In others, we have made accommodations to early elementary, upper-elementary, middle, and high school. The advantage of a single set of non-negotiables across the entire span is that you achieve continuity from pre-K through grade 12. However, in order to achieve this, the non-negotiables have to be somewhat broader. However, one can also modify attributes—for example, dropping "decodes fluently" beyond grade 2, along with its non-negotiables that don't apply beyond that grade except for a handful of struggling readers (one can always keep this attribute going for individual students who haven't yet met the benchmark). If you choose to create sets of non-negotiables for different levels, you can fine-tune them a little more, but I'd recommend trying to create one set and then modifying them only if needed. One way to do this is to insert a modification, as we did in the following example, to insist on daily independent reading in elementary school, acknowledging that we couldn't insist on it in middle and high school:

- Provide frequent (daily, in elementary school) opportunities and encouragement for students to read a substantial amount and to read widely (including self-selected, teacher-prompted material).

Remember that the *instructional activities* can easily be tailored to specific grade levels, so trying to specify different non-negotiables for different grade levels is unnecessary and defeats the purpose of the exercise in the first place.

Instructional Activities

The non-negotiables define the few, critical contributions that teachers need to make in order for students to acquire the literacy attributes. As I said earlier, the instructional activities represent the accommodations needed to address the particular strengths and needs of diverse students, as well as put to good use the craft and expertise of individual teachers. Instructional activities also represent legitimately different instructional methods and materials to achieve common goals. Further, it's the instructional activities that provide the variety so necessary to motivate students across the years. This doesn't mean that teachers can do whatever they like. It means that they should select, either by themselves or in collaboration with colleagues, instructional activities that best implement the non-negotiables. Instructional activities are, by definition, varied, because students' needs are not the same, and no single instructional approach works with all students.

In Chapter One, I shared the non-negotiable instructional contributions created by one school district for the attribute "reads widely." This is a good example to use to show the relationship between non-negotiables and instructional activities. Next, I've listed the original non-negotiables, but this time, I've added underneath a description of instructional activities that support the non-negotiables.

Non-Negotiable Instructional Contributions to Reading Widely:

- Model reading from a variety of printed sources (*genre*— fiction, nonfiction, poetry; content areas; *diversity*—author, culture, gender, topics; *forms of print*—books, magazines, newspapers, documents, electronic media; *purpose*— information, pleasure).

The instructional activities here include selecting the specific books and other media for use in modeling reading widely. What would vary here is the balance between the various sources. So a kindergarten teacher might model reading from a local newspaper, while a middle school teacher might read from the *New York Times*; similarly, a second-grade teacher might read from Scholastic's *Scope*, while a high school teacher reads from the *New Yorker*. The non-negotiable provides the template for a teacher to select the specific materials.

- Make available a substantial amount and a wide variety of printed and electronic material (in classroom, school library).

There has to be a wide range of materials available to teachers and students. It's the principle of accessibility: you can't read what isn't available to you. The challenge here is how best to make materials accessible. In some schools, investing in classroom libraries may be the most effective strategy; it puts materials closest to where students spend most of their time in school. In others, especially with limited funds or where the library or media center is literally in the center of the school, it may make better sense to focus on strengthening the center's collection. Implementing this non-negotiable also implies figuring out ways to connect the collection of materials with both teachers and students.

- Provide frequent (daily, in elementary school) opportunities and encouragement for students to read a substantial amount and to read widely (including self-selected, teacher-prompted material).

Here's where we would expect marked variations across the grade levels in implementing this non-negotiable. For one thing, there's a world of difference between what it means for a pre-kindergartner and a tenth-grader to "read a substantial amount," or even to "read." Thus both the time made available and the nature of the activity itself will vary enormously. Also the balance between self-selected and teacher-prompted choices of reading material needs to be thoughtfully considered, taking into account things like motivation, reading difficulties, and reading interests.

- Provide frequent opportunities for students to share reading experiences.

The emphasis here is on students talking with one another about their reading, leaving the particular techniques up to teachers. For some, simply setting aside time each week for students to talk in small groups about what they are reading would meet this non-negotiable. For others, perhaps, Nancie Atwell's notion of a group share first thing in the morning (Atwell 1987) would do it.

Sources for Instructional Activities

There's no shortage of professional books, practitioner journals, educator magazines, and commercially available programs for teachers to use as sources for instructional activities. In fact, it's almost overwhelming, and keeping up with the latest literature could be a full-time job.

Professional books from major educational publishing houses such as Heinemann, Stenhouse, Scholastic, and Pearson are essential sources. Some of the classics (for example, Regie Routman's *Conversations* [Routman 2000]; Nancie Atwell's *In the Middle* [Atwell 1987]) include time-proven instructional activities across a wide range of language arts. But there are also a number of books that provide wonderful suggestions for teaching specific components, such as spelling (Wilde 1991; Chandler 1999), or comprehension (Keene and Zimmermann 1997; Dorn and Soffos 2005). Still others provide excellent examples of literature circles (Samway and Whang 1995; Daniels 2002; Day et al. 2002).

I also routinely scan the latest catalogues of the professional organizations, including the IRA, the NCTE, the Association for Supervision and Curriculum Development (ASCD), and the NAEYC. All these organizations have practitioner publications that are rich sources of ideas for instructional activities. For example, one of my favorite recent books from ASCD is Marzano's book on building background knowledge (Marzano 2004), and one of my all-time favorites from NCTE is Katie Wood Ray's *Wondrous Words* (Ray 1999).

Of course, educators already know about practitioner journals (for example, *Language Arts*, the *Reading Teacher*, the *English Journal*, *Educational Leadership*, *Young Children*) and magazines (*Instructor*, *K–8*). These are all about instructional activities.

Many of these journals are refereed, and teachers can be sure that instructional activities drawn from them will be worth trying in the classroom.

Finally, colleagues are a great source for instructional activities. Of course, if you are a teacher, you already know that.

Summary

The notion of non-negotiables and instructional activities may be one of the most innovative and challenging aspects of this book. It changes the language arts curriculum from a large list of skills per grade level to a small number of important literacy attributes. It then suggests the few critical things that each and every teacher must provide, as well as suggestions for instructional activities that best implement these non-negotiables.

However, non-negotiables and instructional activities have to be organized and delivered in classrooms, and take into consideration the time available for language arts, and what I call the "containers" in which language arts is delivered. These are what we need to examine next, in Chapter Four.

4

ORGANIZING LANGUAGE
ARTS INSTRUCTION

Most schools have a language arts curriculum that lays out literacy goals or expectations, typically by grade level. But the majority also have commercial reading series (basal readers, anthologies) that provide teachers with a scope and sequence of skills, daily lesson plans, and materials for teachers and students. And there are instructional activities that lie outside the commercial series, such as silent sustained reading, reading and writing workshops, and state test preparation, to name just a few. So teachers have to negotiate between what their district has set as literacy expectations, what the commercial series provides them, and what else they feel is needed in their classroom. This is more of a challenge in elementary and middle school than in high school; the high school curriculum typically is prescribed by district or state examinations, which allow little room for variation except in elective courses.

Language arts instruction can be thought of as being delivered in what I call containers. *Container* is a term that describes the overall structure and organization of the content of language arts instruction, as well as the time allocation to its various parts. Think of a container as a big box in which one can find all the instructional activities, how they are sequenced or arranged, what they teach or engage students in, and what time is allocated for them, both overall and individually. Containers can comprise an entire program from single or multiple vendors, a mix of commercial and teacher-made programs, or entirely teacher-made programs.

In elementary schools, daily language arts instruction ranges from sixty to ninety minutes, sometimes longer. Once the curriculum is departmentalized at about sixth grade or so, language arts is usually relegated to an average of one thirty- to fifty-minute period a day, with possibly an additional period for less able students. The overall time devoted to language arts varies considerably across schools, as does the proportion of time devoted to each of the language arts components.

In terms of how the content of language arts is structured, one grade level's language arts program might be organized around themes, another with a basal reading series or literature anthology, another with separate blocks of time for different components. Further, how literacy instruction is divided between language arts and other subject areas, all of which use receptive and expressive literacy in studying content, plays itself out in different ways across schools and grades.

An attributes framework brings coherence, simplicity, and focus to literacy expectations, and there are strong connections among attributes, instructional contributions, assessment, reporting, and analyzing data. But the framework faces the same challenge as traditional language arts programs, in that there isn't a direct and necessarily obvious connection between the attributes, instructional contributions, and the containers in which it is delivered in the classroom. The important principle here is that whatever container the language arts program is delivered in, what really matters is how it ensures students' progress toward the attributes. That said, some language arts containers seem more suited to this mission than others.

Language Arts Containers

Although literacy attributes and instructional contributions are listed by literacy component (for example, reading, writing), language arts instruction does not have to be organized in this way; in fact, that's the last way I would recommend that it be delivered. However, there's no evidence that would support a single, right way to do so. There are many ways to organize literacy instruction to support students' acquisition of the attributes. Some districts create their own unique containers; most use commercial series and supplement them with what's called homegrown approaches. No Child Left Behind legislation has profoundly influenced the choice of language arts containers in the past few years, so commercial, packaged programs are fast becoming the containers of choice, especially in districts with schools that fail to meet adequate yearly progress on state and federal literacy tests. These programs are also being used increasingly in suburban and more affluent districts that are afraid they might fall short if they don't cover themselves by using programs that are "approved" under NCLB.

Let me review some of the different containers currently in use in elementary, middle, and high school. I've chosen just a few of them to illustrate the notion of containers. What follows is not intended as an exhaustive review. The most widespread container in use across public schools is still the *basal reading* or *literature series* created by the major publishing companies (for example, McGraw-Hill, Harcourt Brace, Scott, Foresman). For a while, in the mid-1980s, there was a slight decline in the use of these series, as literature-based and theme-based containers thrived, but since No Child Left Behind came into being, these series and many smaller "research-based" packaged programs have enjoyed a resurgence as the containers of choice.

A typical reading basal is organized around units that focus on literacy skills, with passages for students to read, discuss, and respond to, plus directed skills lessons for teachers to teach and students to practice. One notable change over the past few years is that these series contain more "real" literature than they did in the past, but they now also contain more direct instruction of basic decoding skills than they did before as well. Sometimes, as I walk through classrooms, I think I am transported back to the days of Science Research Associates (SRA) "learning labs," with their little instructional cards in different colors.

Another container is what is called *balanced literacy*. Although this term means different things to different educators, it is most closely associated with the work of Fountas and Pinnell and their guided reading approach (Fountas and Pinnell 1996; Fountas and Pinnell 2006). Although one might be excused for thinking that guided reading lessons look strikingly like reading group instruction in a traditional basal reader, they are different because they use what are called leveled books. Although this approach is popular in the early grades, the authors also offer *Guiding Reading and Writers* (Fountas and Pinnell 2000) for teaching both reading and writing in the upper-elementary grades.

In a *theme-based* approach to language arts, students read, write, listen, speak, view, and represent within a content-rich, integrated framework. In this approach, language arts is treated the same way it is in the real world—not as a subject area but as a means for understanding content and expressing ideas about content. I have to confess my own bias toward this container for language arts; I've advocated for it for many years and have written about it (Walmsley, Camp et al. 1992; Walmsley 1994), as have others (Beane 1991; Manning, Manning et al. 1994; Pappas, Kiefer et al. 1999). A variation on themes is *inquiry-based* instruction (Short, Schroeder et al. 1996; Chancer and Rester-Zodrow 1997; Whitin and Whitin 1997). Theme-based approaches have waxed and waned over the last two centuries (yes, it was popular in the 1860s), but currently we are in a waning period. This is surprising, since content-rich language arts programs are strongly advocated by both progressive and conservative educators.

A *literature-based* approach to language arts is a close cousin to the theme container. It organizes language arts around the study of literature. This is essentially the container of choice for middle and high school English programs, but it has also been popular in elementary schools (Walmsley and Walp 1990; Walmsley and Walp 1991; Walmsley 1992). Some instructional strategies have helped institutionalize this approach across the grades, including grand conversations (Peterson and Eeds 1990), literature circles (Samway and Whang 1995; Daniels 2002), envisioning literature (Langer 1995), and literature units (Moss 1990; Moss 1994; Moss 1996).

A *genre* approach could be said to be a direct descendant of a literature-based method; it uses literary genres as the basis for organizing language arts instruction. Genre studies have always been popular at the secondary level, but increasingly, organizing writing instruction around genres (memoir, poetry, reports, personal narratives, journals) and even reading (fiction, nonfiction, poetry) have become quite common in elementary schools. Aligning genres in both reading and writing is quite a challenge, and I've noticed that most schools tend to keep them separate. For a long time, genre studies in the elementary grades were relatively brief writing projects devoted to genres such as poetry, biography, or reports. Recently, the idea of organizing an entire writing program around genres (Calkins 2003) or a significant part of it (Youngs and Barone 2007) has become a popular container for this aspect of language arts.

A *workshop* approach emphasizes reading or writing, or a combination of these. This approach, first popularized by authors such as Donald Murray (Murray 1978) and Donald Graves (Graves 1983) in the mid-1970s and further developed by numerous authors (Calkins and Harwayne 1990; Harwayne 1992) focuses on the craft of writing and reading in a workshop setting. Typically, the two kinds of workshops are separate from each other (there'll be time set aside for writer's workshop, and a different time for reader's workshop). However, Katie Wood Ray (Ray 1999; Ray 2001) has pioneered a form of writer's workshop that fully integrates the two processes; it represents to me a truly innovative container for reader's and writer's workshops.

In middle and high school, English/language arts instruction is much more standardized in terms of the time allocation and the containers. The only variation in time allocation is the length of class periods and how they are scheduled on a weekly basis (for example, offered daily or on a rotating basis; many shorter periods or fewer longer ones). As far as containers are concerned, most middle and high schools use the university model of semester- or year-length courses. Anthologies and textbooks predominate in secondary school.

Middle schools do vary, according to the grades that they cover (for example, 6, 7, and 8 or just 7 and 8), and especially where they decide to make the break between self-contained classrooms and departmentalized structures. I have seen as many sixth grades that are self-contained as departmentalized, and have never fully understood other than historical precedent why a district ended up with one or the other.

But there's one other language arts container, although strictly speaking, it isn't a language arts program: *literacy across the curriculum*. In the elementary grades, this is typically integrated into the regular classroom. At about sixth grade, with content areas taught by content-area teachers, it gets separated from regular English classes. There seems to be some uncertainty about how literacy should be incorporated across subject areas. I notice a trend in elementary schools to "borrow" time from science and social studies to increase literacy instruction, which not only neglects important content knowledge but also may decrease the kinds of reading and writing that are specific to content areas (for example, comprehension and composition of nonfiction text). At the secondary level, I see too often missed opportunities to engage students in the kinds of literacy that most relate to specific content areas, such as viewing and representing in art, science, and social studies. As a container for language arts, literacy across the curriculum seems to have more potential than is currently recognized or realized.

Of course, it's rare that any of these containers are used exclusively as the organizing structure of language arts in individual classrooms, let alone across whole school districts. I have seen schools that have bought into writers' workshops in such a committed way that they permeated the entire elementary grades, fully implementing non-negotiables for writing but only partially implementing reading non-negotiables. I've seen districts that had an overall literature-based structure, but if you examined individual classrooms, you'd see huge variations in the way the approach was implemented. This is even true of basal reading series, which give the appearance of consistency within and across the grades. When you look closely at how they are implemented, there is always considerable variation in both what is covered and omitted and what is added by individual teachers.

Comparison of Containers

All the containers described here will work with an attributes framework, but they each have issues. The most significant is that teachers will need to make adjustments, some quite large, to ensure that the instructional activities implement the non-negotiables. This isn't surprising, given that neither commercial language arts programs nor homegrown approaches were designed within an attributes framework. Yet teachers are used to supplementing their basal reading series to ensure that aspects of language arts they deem important are included in their program. For example, many teachers replace the writing components of their basal reading series with other approaches such as 6+1 Traits (Culham 2003) or writer's workshop (Ray 2001).

When you look at the various containers from an attributes perspective, however, a theme- or inquiry-based approach appears to offer significant advantages. It folds the language arts activities into meaningful content and folds literacy skills into the activities. For example, a student might be reading books and other material to learn about a topic (say, the ecology of a town dump, or how submarines work, or rocks and minerals, or the concept of survival). The reading material may represent a range of genres (fiction, nonfiction), different formats (books, magazines, Web sites, newspapers), and levels of difficulty. Within each reading, there'll be opportunities for decoding word meanings, comprehending, and comparing across texts. Explicit teaching of literacy skills could precede, accompany, or follow these experiences. And writing, speaking, listening, viewing, and representing can easily be integrated with the reading, because they each can be connected to the topics under study. In other words, this approach comfortably includes all the attributes within a single container. By integrating them and connecting them to content, language arts are taught efficiently and purposefully. Further, a theme-based approach is an ideal vehicle for exploring and relating content areas, because it's the content that holds everything together. The downside is that creating and managing themes or inquiries takes a lot of preparation, and there's always the fear that required literacy skills haven't been covered or their treatment is haphazard. And in middle and high schools, the logistics of integrated units in a highly departmentalized school, with a regimented curriculum and schedule, frequently sabotage even the most concerted efforts to create and carry them out.

Each of the other containers I've described may represent excellent examples of best practices but, by themselves, only partially address the attributes. I see them more as mini-containers—in other words, collections of instructional activities that are ideally suited for implementing specific non-negotiable instructional contributions. For example, a "balanced literacy" approach, which typically involves the use of Fountas and Pinnell's guided reading, offers a thoroughly modern pedagogy for teaching decoding, comprehension, and literary understanding that makes traditional reading groups obsolete. Although Fountas and Pinnell also offer writing instruction, balanced literacy as it is currently conceived probably isn't the best container for balancing *all* the language arts. Speaking, listening, viewing, and representing are not given the attention they need.

Similarly, a genre container for reading or writing represents an innovative approach to developing reading comprehension or composing strategies (and even more so when they are taught together). Genre containers offer unique ways to help students understand the underlying structures of different kinds of texts, which in turn improves reading comprehension and also develops writing skills. But if you chart how well they cover non-negotiables across all the language arts, they would need to be supplemented quite significantly to achieve this.

In sum, unless a theme- or inquiry-based container could be constructed so that teachers wouldn't have to develop so much of their own language arts instructional activities (a contradiction in terms, especially for inquiries, which by definition follow the students' questions and interests), there are no current containers that slide easily and comfortably into an attributes framework.

Reflections on Containers and Attributes

It's important to remember that commercial reading programs and approaches offered by professional authors are simply tools to use to help teachers accomplish their language arts goals. They are not the curriculum, and they are certainly not the goals. Programs and approaches have to be evaluated in terms of what aspects of literacy they cover, how well they cover them, and how they help students achieve literacy expectations. In the case of an attributes framework, these goals are represented by the attributes, and the curriculum is represented by the non-negotiables and the instructional activities. If you think about it, a basal reading series is a collection of instructional activities and materials. So, too, are all the containers I've described. Although the framework is neutral with respect to the kind of container used for organizing and teaching language arts, it is not neutral with respect to what the containers need to deliver.

The framework insists on the following for all containers:

- They implement the non-negotiable instructional contributions.
- They provide for successful differentiated instruction.
- They do not inhibit or prevent any other non-negotiables from being carried out.

Modifications must be made if they fail to meet any of these requirements. Just because a publisher of a commercial literacy series *says* their program differentiates instruction does not make it so. Just because they *say* they cover writing does not mean that this is the best approach. Educators should not hesitate to modify or even replace parts of a program in order to provide teachers and students with the best teaching and learning practices that will move students steadily toward the literacy attributes.

Similarly, although the framework is neutral with respect to the allocation of time to language arts, it is not neutral with respect to giving each of the language arts components and each of the attributes sufficient time for both instruction by teachers and sustained engagement by students. Obviously, elementary schools have more time available for language arts, and they need it in order to focus on emergent literacy development. Having 90–120 minutes a day devoted exclusively to language arts is more than reasonable, but how that time should be used to best ensure progress in literacy is still an open question. No one has yet demonstrated the superiority of one allocation method over another, and each method has both pluses and minuses. For example, regrouping certainly allows children with similar needs to be taught together; the downside is that these children have a more fractionated language arts curriculum, and they have less sustained language arts engagement. Schools have to figure out which instructional structures produce the best results *for all students*. Sometimes, research offers valuable assistance. For example, studies examined by the National Reading Panel (NICHD 2000) show that there are diminishing returns in spending too much time on small group instruction on phonemic awareness in the very early grades and that explicit instruction in phonics beyond second grade appears to have relatively little impact on reading comprehension. In one school I have worked with, the kindergartens spend nearly ninety minutes every day teaching phonics, which not only may not advance students' phonic skills; it may actually diminish their comprehension abilities by spending almost no time on anything *but* phonics.

Other organizational issues need attention, including how best to meet the needs of all students, how we might better spread literacy across the curriculum, and how skills get taught in an attributes framework.

Meeting the Needs of All Students

We need to acknowledge the tension between standardizing the curriculum to provide equal access to high-quality literacy instruction and the need for unique literacy experiences and instruction that meet the needs of individual students with different background knowledge and cultural experiences, a range of learning styles, and literacy abilities. In some cases, what will work best for a student is a set of curriculum experiences or literacy strategies that is deliberately *different* from what's provided to other students. This is not an argument for a completely individualized curriculum; it's an acknowledgment that one size does not fit all and that consistency of materials, programs, and containers does not guarantee consistency of results.

Making Better Use of Literacy Across the Curriculum

The other issue here relates to how much of the contribution to the literacy attributes should be made within English/language arts and how much from other subject areas. Yet these contributions must be made if a student is to be fully literate, that is, able to read, think, write, and represent like a scientist, mathematician, artist, musician, sports player, or historian; to interpret primary source documents; to acquire the background knowledge needed to make sense of more complex texts. In this framework, I do not propose that content-area teachers become reading or writing teachers but rather that they be willing to make their contributions in the following ways:

- Focus primarily on deepening and extending students' understanding of their content (this is a huge contribution to literacy, but they might not realize this).
- Engage students in reading, writing, speaking, listening, viewing, and representing that are *intimately connected to the content area* (in art classes, students engage a great deal in

viewing and representing; in science, they engage in scientific writing and reading).

- Respond to students' literacy primarily from the perspective of the subject area (in other words, focus on the scientific content, style, and language of the lab report rather than on writing mechanics).

- Model, value, and encourage students in learning more about the subject area (through reading, taking trips, watching documentaries).

- Create interdisciplinary units that allow both teachers and students to dig in deep into topics that integrate content areas with literature (yes, this is hard to do, but when it can be done, it's a significant contribution).

These suggestions don't just apply to departmentalized classrooms. They are just as valuable for a kindergarten teacher who needs to explore literacy across the curriculum, and they are much easier to pull off.

Teaching Literacy Skills

Emphasizing the few, critical attributes and instructional contributions is very important. Huge lists of skills per grade level look impressive in documents, but the longer the lists, the less likely they will be used to guide daily practice. So where in the framework are skills taught? First, they will be seen in each of the areas, under the non-negotiables. All the traditional skills are there (for example, letter and letter-sound knowledge in reading fluently; spelling, grammar, handwriting in writing mechanics). However, they are not listed by grade level because generally they apply to all grade levels. For example, reading comprehension strategies are the same from first through twelfth grade and beyond. What is different is the complexity of the ideas and the language in the materials being read. The same is true of writing mechanics: punctuation, spelling, and grammar need to be continually taught and applied to writing across the grades. They can't be simply taught at one grade level and assumed to be mastered.

This isn't to suggest that particular skills in reading, writing, speaking, listening, viewing, and representing should not be assigned to particular grade levels to be introduced, perhaps even taught explicitly. It means that everything needed to ensure students' steady progress toward the attributes is taught and experienced whenever it is needed. Skills teaching in this framework is not merely covering specific skills at specific grade levels; it's engaging students in them constantly at ever-increasing levels of sophistication. If a kindergartner is sufficiently advanced in writing that teaching him how to use semicolons is appropriate, then that's what is done. If a seventh grader still can't use periods properly in her writing, then heaven and earth need to be moved to ensure that she does.

Very little of what I have suggested in this section requires a large-scale change in the language arts programs currently being used in a district to be compatible with and take advantage of an attributes framework. But the attributes and non-negotiable instructional contributions provide a template against which programs and approaches can be compared and appropriate adjustments made. For example, the attribute "reads widely" and its instructional contributions can be used to check on the balance of fiction, nonfiction, and poetry in language arts programs from pre-K onward, regardless of the container or containers currently in use. In a theme- or inquiry-based approach, checks could be made to ensure that themes incorporate wide reading (across genres, topics, different kinds of materials, and so on), not necessarily in each theme but overall, across the year. A genre approach might have to be tweaked a little to ensure that genre alone doesn't determine the width of student reading. Here's where literacy across the curriculum could play an important role, by having students read journals, magazines, Web material, and perhaps biographies and fiction related to topics being studied in science and social studies.

In each case, having the attributes and non-negotiables provides teachers and schools with a rational basis for ensuring that the containers they use for language arts are suitably diverse yet make substantial contributions to literacy expectations.

A closing example: my experience in New York schools is that poetry is seriously neglected across the grades, and when students reach high school, this lack of exposure to poetry puts many of them at a huge disadvantage in state regents examinations. If every grade level made appropriate contributions to students' poetry exposure and understanding, regardless of whether themes, genres, or basal readers organized the language arts instruction, high school teachers wouldn't be desperately trying to catch students up.

Summary

Most elementary schools across the nation organize their language arts programs around commercially available reading or literature series ("basals," as they are called in elementary schools, "textbooks" in middle and high school). But there are many alternative approaches available, such as theme- or inquiry-based, genre, and workshop containers. An attributes framework does not require a particular container for language arts instruction, but it does insist that containers implement the non-negotiables, and give adequate time and attention to all the literacy attributes. Most importantly, though, programs and approaches are for implementing a language arts curriculum; they are not the curriculum itself. An attributes framework provides the curriculum (in other words, what the goals are and the critical instructional contributions), while the containers provide the materials and organization of the daily classroom activities.

5

INSTRUCTIONAL SUPPORT FOR STRUGGLING STUDENTS

It's hard to imagine that fifty years ago, there were no reading or special education teachers in the United States. Now specialists of all kinds proliferate in elementary and secondary schools, and the term *instructional support* covers a wide range of programs that provide additional help to students who struggle to learn.

As far as literacy is concerned, there are two major instructional support approaches: reading and special education. Remedial or "compensatory" reading got its start with Title 1 of the Elementary and Secondary Education Act of 1965. Special education took off with the passing of PL94-142, the Education for All Handicapped Children Act (EHA) in 1975. Since then, Title 1 has morphed into Chapter 1 and back into Title 1 again and more recently has been subsumed into the No Child Left Behind legislation of 2002. EHA has morphed into the Individuals with Disabilities Education Act (IDEA) and has undergone several changes, the latest and most far-reaching of which is the 2004 reauthorization. IDEA2004 changes the entire basis not just for special education but for all instructional support in the elementary years.

One of the interesting things about both remedial reading and special education is that even though their origins are quite dissimilar, their instructional focus is similar—primarily reading and mathematics. Remedial reading comes from the War on Poverty and started as a mechanism to compensate for students' inadequate literacy experiences before coming to school. Special education derives from civil rights principles that insist that all children be provided with the services they are entitled to. Further, the basis for their funding has been different from the start. Title 1 and Chapter 1 programs have been funded on the basis of poverty indicators in a district (for example, numbers of children eligible for free lunches), while special education programs are funded on the basis of the educational needs of individual students, as determined by testing.

Finally, for reasons that aren't at all clear, the two approaches are often differentiated in terms of instructional philosophy, with remedial reading taking a somewhat eclectic approach to instruction, whereas special education has taken a much more behaviorist approach. This is reinforced in the training of the two kinds of specialists. Remedial reading teachers have traditionally been trained alongside classroom teachers in programs that have a fairly broad set of courses, including the teaching of developmental reading, as well as remedial. On the other hand, special education teachers have often been trained with only one or two courses in reading required in their program of study. This is, I admit, changing, but even in the programs in my own university, the training of special educators still is dominated by a behaviorist philosophy, while literacy specialists (the current name for reading specialists) are trained within a much more constructivist philosophy.

In schools, it isn't hard to see these differences in action. First, the reading specialists are often more closely connected to classroom literacy instruction than the special educators, both instructionally and organizationally, although many schools are now trying what is called "collaborative" classrooms, where a mix of regular and special needs children are collaboratively taught by a regular and special education teacher, or a consultant model in which specialists "push-in" to regular classrooms. In most schools where I've done audits, a common complaint by special educators is that they feel disconnected from the schools in which they work. I also hear complaints from both literacy specialists and special educators that they provide similar services to students yet rarely collaborate with each other. Of course, this lack of collaboration is almost guaranteed by the way in which students get into instructional support in the first place. Being referred to remedial reading or math is often as simple as failing a state literacy or math test. In New York State, for example, students performing at Level 1 or 2 (that is, below expectations) on a state examination in grades 3 through 8 must be offered instructional support. They also can be referred for additional support in literacy by classroom teachers. The process for receiving special education services is much more elaborate, and it's governed by strict legal requirements.

When I first started developing the attributes approach, districts in New York State were not required to have the same literacy standards for all students in the district, so my early projects typically excluded special education students but always included remedial reading students. This wasn't my choice; it was the district's choice. From the beginning, I had the idea that although students had differing abilities, backgrounds, and experiences, our expectations for what I called "genuine literacy" should apply to everyone, even though outcomes would vary. So I was disappointed each time the decision was made to exclude special education from the projects.

What changed everything, in New York State at any rate, was the introduction of the state learning standards and the state's insistence that they apply to all students. At first, there were all kinds of modifications, alternate testing strategies, and reporting procedures that basically allowed school districts to exclude special needs students from the results. But in each revision, the noose has been drawn tighter, and now, not only are all students included in the standards, in the state assessment system, and in the reporting of results, but the state has started identifying schools that have not made improvements in meeting a certain criteria for percentages of special education students passing the assessments. Certainly, the outcomes in New York State are heavily weighted toward academic literacy, and many (including me) have qualms about this, given that literacy in the real world beyond school is much broader than the literacy of school examinations. However, no one in New York State schools can now argue that students with special needs should be excluded from a district's literacy expectations and curriculum. This is also true of students whose first language is not English, whose numbers are increasing rapidly and who account for significant percentages of students failing to meet state literacy standards.

The other thing that's changed is that many special education training programs have started to define literacy more broadly and to insist that students preparing for careers in special education take more courses in literacy. I also see a softening of what was once a fairly rigid adherence to behaviorist teaching principles. There are still marked differences between the training of special educators and literacy specialists, but they are far less pronounced than they used to be. We have hands-on experience with this at the University at Albany: we created two master's degrees that combine both special education and literacy. In fact, these joint programs may be one of the best ways to break down philosophical and pedagogical barriers between literary specialists and special educators. But thus far, courses in these programs are not jointly taught; rather, the programs merely require course work from two separate departments. In this way, perhaps, we mirror—or perpetuate—the dual system that exists in public schools.

The history of both remedial reading and special education does not augur well for either of them in terms of long-term, successful results (Walmsley and Allington 1995). It does not appear that No Child Left Behind, whose primary mission is to help struggling readers, has markedly improved the situation, either (see Fuller et al. 2007). So now our attention and hopes turn toward the most recent initiative, Response to Intervention (RTI), which schools in New York State (at least) have to implement by 2012. It remains to be seen how RTI improves the quality of instructional support, especially how it reduces the numbers of students at risk of literacy failure.

So what does instructional support look like in an attributes framework, and how does it meet the needs of struggling students? And what are the implications of the new RTI framework? How might RTI and an attributes approach work together?

Instructional Support Within the Current Attributes Framework

An attributes framework challenges the traditionally narrow definition of literacy used in both remedial reading and special education. While it's true that what used to be called a reading specialist is now called a literacy specialist, the focus of instruction in Title 1 is still heavily weighted toward reading, perhaps even more so because of Reading First, with far less emphasis on writing, listening, speaking, viewing, and representing. Special educators still tend to focus on decoding skills and literal comprehension, as well as on mechanics in writing.

An attributes framework does not challenge intentional teaching of decoding skills, but it does challenge a strict hierarchy of skills acquisition and teaching, and especially it challenges the idea that literacy should primarily be defined as reading. Instead, it advocates supporting children's development of all aspects of literacy, because they all contribute to each other. The ability to understand what is read is not simply a question of being able to decode. It's also a function of accumulated background knowledge, the acquisition of comprehension strategies, and the contributions made through developing writing, listening, speaking, viewing, and representing skills. Thus an attributes framework insists that instructional support specialists attend to all critical components of literacy.

Second, an attributes framework provides instructional support specialists with a set of literacy expectations that can guide their assessment of students' strengths and weaknesses across all aspects of literacy. In the case of Title 1 specialists, these expectations provide a sound basis for programming. For special education specialists, they provide the basis for generating individualized instructional plans (IEPs). Clearly, struggling students need instruction and experiences that are more focused and scaffolded than they receive in regular classrooms; otherwise they wouldn't be struggling. But unless the assessment starts with an appraisal of where the student performs in relation to the literacy expectations of the student population as a whole, whatever ends up as the student's remedial plan is likely to be biased toward what the specialist (or sometimes the IEP software) defines as literacy. Indeed, you don't have to look at more than a dozen IEPs in a given district to figure out how narrow the focus of instruction is going to be for students with the most pressing needs in literacy.

Third, the assessment phase of an attributes framework insists that the report card conveys to parents how well the student is progressing toward the attributes. Here is one of the biggest departures from traditional approaches with struggling students. The problem is that there's increasing reluctance to share bad news with parents about their children, so instead of saying where the child is relative to the district's literacy expectations, teachers and specialists tend to either report progress in a curriculum or say how well the child is doing in materials at his or her level. So parents are sometimes left wondering if their children are actually performing on grade level or simply doing as well as they can, given lowered expectations. What's interesting is that if a report card actually covers the full range of literacy attributes, it's very rare that any child is weak across all literacy attributes, even though he or she may be struggling with many of them. So the picture is never as bleak as educators fear. In districts where we have instituted an attributes report card for all students, instructional support specialists have been quite surprised that parents appreciate being told the truth about where their child is in relation to district expectations and are relieved that the school understands and uses the child's strengths to support progress in areas of concern.

The bottom line here is that instructional support is only partially about what goes on in remedial or special education classrooms or in programs outside of school. Most struggling students spend less than 10 percent of their instructional day outside of regular classrooms. Until we can rely on instructional support programs to bring struggling students up to the literacy levels of their peers in much better percentages than they presently do, the contribution of regular classroom instruction and the contributions of both over a sustained period, starting even before students arrive in kindergarten, are going to be necessary. In an attributes approach, these contributions start at birth, not after a student has begun to show signs of inadequate literacy development in kindergarten or first grade.

In sum, an attributes approach changes instructional support programs in several ways. Most important, literacy attributes become the starting and ending points for all students identified as needing instructional support. What this means is that the literacy attributes assessments used with all students are used initially to make decisions about what instructional support is needed and who is to provide it. These same assessments are used to determine when a student no longer needs support. However, additional assessments are used to explore students' areas of difficulty. For example, if a kindergartner demonstrates slow growth in decoding fluency (as measured, say, on the DRA), additional assessments would be carried out to determine his or her knowledge of letters and letter sounds, phonemic awareness, sight words, and so on. Similarly, if a third-grader exhibited very weak comprehension skills in an Individualized Reading Inventory (IRI), further assessment of the child's comprehension strategies would need to be done. The same would be true of writing, so that more specific information about the child's composing strategies (for example, generating, developing, and organizing ideas), language and style (for example, word choice), and mechanics (for example, spelling, grammar, punctuation) could be determined for instructional purposes. The advantage of starting with more general assessments of each child's literacy abilities is that it always gives the instructional support specialists a clear idea of each student's overall literacy strengths and areas of weakness and, most important, what the end goal of instructional support should be. If these are followed up with more detailed assessments in the weak areas, specialists will have a good working knowledge of what a struggling student needs and what strengths can be used to build areas of weakness.

An attributes framework does not prescribe the particular instructional practices to be used in support programs, any more than it does so in regular classrooms. Nor does it insist on particular organizational structures, although maintaining close ties with the regular classroom teachers is essential, because each struggling reader's support comes equally from specialists and classroom teachers. Of course, the easiest way to coordinate this support is to have specialists push-in to regular classrooms, although the setting for delivery of services does not necessarily lead to, much less guarantee, coordination. However, there are also advantages to pull-out classes, where specialists can work with struggling students without the distractions of regular classrooms. The important point here is that the classroom teachers and support specialists work together to provide appropriate instruction and experiences that best meet struggling students' needs.

How students end up in Title 1 or special education classes is largely a matter of the legislation and the district's practices for referrals. An attributes framework doesn't interfere with these procedures, except to insist that each child's current status with respect to literacy attributes be an integral part of the referral. And there are other regulations that affect such referrals, such as the ones I've described earlier: failure on a state literacy assessment. The criteria for referrals are much stricter for special education than Title 1, but all referrals are influenced by parents and teachers. Using the literacy attributes to guide the referral process ensures at least that instructional support is offered to students who struggle in areas that matter to the district, and they provide a rational basis for both entry into and graduation from instructional support.

RTI and an Attributes Framework

The RTI legislation challenges traditional approaches to instructional support by shifting the emphasis from what's wrong with the student to what's wrong with the instruction they have been provided. But it also lends significant support to an attributes approach. By putting the emphasis on instruction, it challenges classroom teachers, literacy specialists, and special educators to work together to find instructional approaches that actually produce measurable results on valid assessments. No such requirements have been in place for either Title 1 or Special Education (although there are requirements for attaining IEP goals). Further, it adopts an organizational strategy that mirrors an attributes approach: setting goals, aligning instruction to them, tracking progress toward them, and analyzing data to inform instruction. And it places significant onus on classroom instruction "intervention" by the classroom teacher before shifting responsibility to specialists.

In *No Quick Fix* (Allington and Walmsley 2007), we argue for a unified approach to instructional support, with a heavy emphasis on the expertise of well-trained specialists, regardless of the funding source. More recently, Allington, in *What Really Matters for Struggling Readers: Designing Research-based Programs* (Allington 2006), has argued that we should be extending best classroom practices into instructional support programs. As the principles and practices of RTI become clearer, however, I think its overall approach to instructional support extends the concept of unified instructional support in substantial ways.

There are several RTI models in the professional literature (Fuchs and Fuchs 2006; Fuchs and Fuchs 2001; Fuchs, Mock et al. 2003). I am particularly impressed with the approach to RTI taken by my colleagues Frank Vellutino and Donna Scanlon. They have developed an RTI model and subjected it to rigorous experimental testing in the field; thus far, significant reductions in the numbers of students who struggle with reading in the early grades have been produced (Vellutino, Scanlon et al. 2006). The Vellutino/Scanlon model (I'll refer to it as VS-RTI) derives from a principled, research-based approach to early literacy intervention, but I especially like the way that it offers school districts an overall framework that guides the selection of students for interventions of increasing degrees of intensity, the nature of the interventions themselves, criteria for "graduating" students, and assessments for keeping track of student growth across time.

Unlike Reading First, which provides only training and programs for instructional support, the approach offered by Vellutino and Scanlon is comprehensive, in that it assigns different roles and instructional responsibilities based on the severity of students' needs and their response to instruction thus far. It also encompasses all instructional support programs in a unified way, while emphasizing connections to the core instructional program.

The VS-RTI approach challenges the traditional assumption that students' literacy difficulties are primarily the result of a gap between their "intelligence" and their "achievement." Instead, students' literacy difficulties are assumed to be the result of instruction that has not met their needs. So instead of placing the blame for inadequate literacy growth on the child's shoulders, it challenges educators to provide high-quality instruction and adapt that instruction, based on how students respond to it.

The approach also articulates different levels, or tiers, of instructional support:

- Tier 1 provides small group instruction in the regular classroom (starting in kindergarten) for the lowest 30 percent of children in specific aspects of literacy and taught by the classroom teacher. The purpose of this instruction would be to accelerate the growth of these children in early literacy skills.

- Tier 2 provides very small group specialized instruction for those children in Tier 1 whose growth was slow or nonexistent, taught by a specialist.

- Tier 3 provides one-on-one specialized instruction for those children in Tier 2 whose growth was slow or nonexistent, again taught by a specialist.

- And finally, although Vellutino and Scanlon don't explicitly refer to this as Tier 4, this level is reserved for those very few children whose progress in Tier 3 has been nonexistent. This tier, basically, is referral to special education.

The approach relies on reliable and valid pre-assessment, on continuous monitoring of literacy progress, and faculty or specialists with the knowledge and expertise to carry out the instruction. No packaged programs are employed; instead, the approach relies on good organization and high-quality teaching that is sensitive to the specific needs of struggling students.

What makes the approach different from existing approaches is that it is highly organized, both within and across the grades. Students are observed and pretested in kindergarten. They are provided appropriate literacy experiences and instruction within the regular kindergarten classroom, but as they show signs of not making adequate progress, the system of tiered interventions kicks in. Because the approach is based on providing instruction that meets students' needs, there is no lowering of standards or expectations ("Well, this girl comes from a poor home, and her parents don't support her," or, "This child has a learning disability, so we can't expect much, can we?"). In fact, as the student moves from tier to tier (an admission that instruction isn't working), the instruction has to be more individualized and tailored to his or her individual needs, hence the reduction in group size until one-to-one instruction is the sole means of delivering support.

Another feature of this approach is that if it works, fewer and fewer students will be receiving Tier 3 and Tier 4 (special education) instruction, so a district will be able to afford instruction in smaller and smaller groups. In a way, what's happening here is making more appropriate instructional contributions early, with primarily regular classroom teachers, while reserving the best-trained and most highly qualified specialists for the decreasing number of students whose learning difficulties are highly resistant to instruction.

The VS-RTI model, as I have suggested earlier, cannot be simply adopted as a "program." However, it can be adopted as an approach, starting with its procedures for identifying students in need of Tier 1 intervention in kindergarten and beginning the process of reorganizing the entire instructional supports for literacy.

Although I think a tiered approach to instructional support promises to change the instructional support landscape, there are some issues yet to be resolved. Clearly, Vellutino and Scanlon have shown that using a highly organized and carefully monitored approach, along with instructional techniques based soundly on research, many more students can read successfully than before. However, these results have been obtained under conditions (for example, substantial federal funding, specialized training) that may be hard to duplicate in schools. The model thus far has also concentrated largely on decoding skills.

The issue of funding is particularly relevant in schools with proportionately large numbers of students struggling with literacy. There are costs associated with training or retraining of teachers and specialists, with new materials, and with record keeping. There may also be costs associated with hiring new specialists, especially to cover instructional support in the upper-elementary, middle, and high schools, whereas RTI is implemented in K–3. RTI will address the needs of incoming kindergartners, but struggling students already in the pipeline also have to be supported. It looks as though some relief will come to school districts in the form of the ability to use a portion of Title 1 funds for RTI, but the issue of where districts can find all the funds to pay for RTI is still very much up in the air.

The issue of training doesn't only involve costs; it also raises the question about whether teachers and specialists already in a school district have the capacity to take on new and demanding roles. Tier 3 and Tier 4 intervention demands specialists with extraordinary expertise. They have to succeed where Tier 1 and Tier 2 interventions have yielded little or no progress. If intervention were merely purchasing packaged programs, this might not be a problem, but Tiers 3 and 4 require highly skilled specialists.

Third, the narrow focus of current RTI models is a two-edged sword. By restricting the focus to reading and even further to primarily decoding skills, it becomes much easier to implement and produce measurable results. But if a district's literacy expectations include the full range of reading behaviors plus writing, listening, speaking, viewing, and representing, RTI becomes much harder to carry out. For example, suppose a district had the following reading attributes as expectations.

- Decodes/Reads fluently (applies appropriate reading strategies, knows conventions of print, demonstrates phonemic awareness, identifies letters and letter sounds, knows sight words)
- Understands what is read (understands informational and literary text, understands big ideas, has an extensive reading vocabulary, applies effective comprehension strategies)
- Reads expressively
- Reads widely

The first and third of these is extensively covered in the VS-RTI model, and there is some attention paid to comprehension. Adding the others means that each would have to be assessed to establish benchmarks and to make decisions about referrals. Each would have to be included in Tier 1 through Tier 4 intervention. And each would have to be included in the progress monitoring and be taken into account when deciding when a student no longer needed intervention. Unless decoding fluency unlocks all of these reading behaviors, I cannot see how they can reasonably be excluded.

But I also would want to make a strong case for including writing attributes:

- Communicates ideas effectively
- Organizes and fully develops writing
- Uses effective language/style
- Uses correct/appropriate mechanics (spelling, grammar, punctuation/capitalization, presentation/handwriting)

You can see how adding writing to the mix complicates things even more. True, the VS-RTI model does address some aspects of writing mechanics (for example, encoding/spelling). While I fully understand the rationale for focusing primarily on reading skills, I also have qualms about neglecting other important literacy attributes.

How RTI and an Attributes Framework Can Work Together

It is clear from the discussion that an RTI model offers both instructional and organizational promise to the decades-old quandary of how best to implement instructional support. Let me offer some tentative thoughts about how RTI and an attributes framework can work together to accomplish more than either can do on its own.

For me, the great strength of the VS-RTI model lies in its tiered approach, which lays out a scheme for increasingly sophisticated instruction for students who are not benefiting from earlier interventions. It does this in a way that ensures that students' difficulties are identified early and remediated first with best-practice instruction within the regular classroom. It also insists that if the student progresses to Tier 2 and beyond, the student is receiving high-quality instruction in the classroom. This model practices the "It's our responsibility" principle of *No Quick Fix* (Allington and Walmsley 2007), and it continues the Title 1 commitment to "supplement, not supplant" regular classroom practice. It also offers rigorous, research-based instruction for both classrooms, especially instructional support.

What the attributes framework adds to VS-RTI is including other critical aspects of reading, as well as essential components of other language arts (writing, listening, speaking, viewing, and representing). How can these be merged? One way is to start earlier than kindergarten. As pre-K becomes more universal, what is currently being done in kindergarten can be started in pre-K. However, if a district either offers preschool classes itself or partners with community-based organizations (for example, Head

Start, Even Start, private preschools, Literacy Volunteers), getting an even earlier start is a viable proposition. One of the districts I have been working with, Ossining Union Free School District, has embraced an attributes framework starting with infants. Adding up to four years' worth of literacy contributions makes a huge difference.

Another is to develop screening measures that provide baseline data on students' acquisition of the literacy attributes (in viewing, representing, reading, writing, speaking, and listening). This does, I admit, add complexity and time to the screening measures, but once implemented, ways will be found to streamline this process. (As I have mentioned elsewhere, the first time a new assessment procedure is put in place, it seems overwhelming. Subsequently, it doesn't seem nearly as complicated or burdensome.)

A third way that attributes help RTI is to bridge the gap between the intensive focus on a narrow set of literacy strategies and the broader literacy expectations of pre-K through grade 12. RTI instruction rightly has a narrow focus, but its effectiveness lies ultimately in how well it accelerates a student's literacy development toward wider literacy achievements. I find it interesting how well some of the approaches deemed "to work" by the U.S. Department of Education's Clearinghouse (Institute of Education Sciences 2007) succeed in meeting small literacy goals (for example, alphabet knowledge) and how few can be shown to have sustained effects on larger literacy goals (for example, overall reading achievement). The challenge of both an attributes framework and RTI models is to meet both short-term and long-term goals. An attributes framework helps RTI understand what is meant by the larger literacy goals.

Finally, an attributes framework ensures that regular classrooms engage students in activities and instruction that make up the "other" part of a struggling student's literacy experiences. RTI cannot succeed any more than any other instructional support approach, if students are not properly engaged in high-quality core components of language arts in their regular classrooms. In fact, if the regular classroom experiences are narrow or of poor quality, no amount of intervention by highly qualified specialists will compensate for them. It is no accident that Reading Recovery, now finally recognized as an effective instructional support approach, assumes that its students will have rich core experiences in the regular classroom.

Summary

In sum, RTI offers a viable framework for addressing the needs of struggling readers in the early grades and already has demonstrated remarkable results in carefully controlled studies (Vellutino, Scanlon et al. 2006). It will be a challenge to replicate these findings when school districts implement RTI without substantial funding or professional development to upgrade the expertise of classroom teachers and specialists. Nonetheless, RTI fits well within an attributes framework with its tiered approach, careful monitoring, and research-based pedagogy. What an attributes framework brings to RTI, however, are the broader literacy behaviors that are the ultimate goal of the focus on narrower literacy skills. The attributes framework also challenges RTI models to include components of language arts other than reading, especially given how much they contribute to reading achievement.

6

LANGUAGE ARTS ASSESSMENT

I am always surprised how much literacy assessment goes on in schools, yet how little seems to be known about the literacy status and progress of students toward literacy goals. For example, I've never encountered anyone in a school district who didn't think that students should have read a lot and have read across a variety of genres. Yet when I ask a question like, "How many students would you say haven't read very much?" I notice that individual teachers can readily answer it, but no one can answer it for the whole school because no one is actually gathering these data across the grades. Some teachers keep track of their students' reading, but it's rarely a requirement that everyone does. But the same is true even in areas like reading fluency. If I ask for data on students' sight word knowledge or their decoding level on measures like the DRA, I find that some teachers gather it, or it's reported on individual report cards, but it generally isn't kept track of across schools or across years. On the other hand, test scores from standardized reading achievement tests or state-mandated English/language arts assessments are instantly available and often have been microanalyzed by district administrators, state agencies, or commercial test companies. But when I ask teachers how these assessments relate to their literacy goals, they tell me the results usually come too late to be of any use and don't give useful information anyway. There is no widespread agreement on what should be assessed, how to gather the evidence, and how to report and analyze it. Moreover, what evidence is gathered tends to be haphazard and so inconsistently analyzed as to render it unhelpful at best, uninterpretable at worst.

Literacy Assessment Principles

In a literacy attributes framework, assessment plays a critical role in keeping track of students' progress toward the literacy attributes, but it also provides the basis for individual report cards, as well as the data needed to improve instruction. The most important principle here is that a district knows where students are relative to *all* the literacy attributes, not just those that are easy to measure or those that are "covered" by existing standardized or mandated assessments. Thus if "reads widely" is a literacy attribute, then *all* teachers will keep track of the amount and breadth of students' reading; they will then report individually to students and their parents and collectively to the school or district. As a consequence, individual teachers, as well as school administrators, can readily answer the question I posed earlier ("How many students would you say haven't read very much?"); parents can be informed about whether their child "reads widely," and the district can analyze both aggregated and disaggregated data on how well—at or across grade levels—this attribute is being met.

Before addressing the pragmatic question about how teachers can and should keep track of an attribute like "reads widely," let me elaborate on the assessment principles I mentioned in Chapter One.

1. *We need to know where all students are, relative to all the literacy attributes.* This is a daunting proposition. But think about the inescapable logic that sits behind it. A district articulates a number of literacy expectations for all students, pre-K through grade 12. It has deliberately focused on the most critical literacy attributes. So shouldn't it be willing—in fact eager—to gather data to show where each student is, relative to the attributes, and how much progress is being made by both individuals (to report to them and their parents), as well as groups of students (to see how well students as a whole are progressing across the grades)?

If a district is serious about its literacy expectations, it has to be able to report these data to students, parents, and the school community. Otherwise, what's the point of having expectations? Given the old adage of what gets assessed gets taught, even a half-hearted attempt to assess progress toward literacy expectations will encourage progress toward them.

When I raise this proposition in school districts, no one questions the logic of assessing literacy attributes. But the moment we start talking about actually doing it, all sorts of objections arise: we already have too many assessments; surely we can use existing assessments to tell us about literacy attributes; it can't be done in middle and high school because of the workload, and so on. All reasonable concerns, I admit, but if they are left unconfronted, inevitably more than half the attributes will not be assessed, and these will remain as desired outcomes but attained only haphazardly.

I do not underestimate the difficulties of keeping track of and reporting student progress toward *all* the attributes, but as will be seen later in this chapter, it is possible to do, and I'll share examples of how it can be done.

2. All *literacy assessments should relate to, and provide information on, each student's progress toward the literacy attributes.* This is the flip side of the first principle. It sounds so obvious, but when I look carefully at the assessments typically used in schools, I routinely find assessments that only tangentially measure important literacy achievement. Often specific measures of noncritical aspects of literacy take up so much time that there's no room for anything else. One of the first tasks in the assessment phase of implementing an attributes framework is to examine all the assessments currently used for tracking progress in literacy and really understand what they are measuring and, more important, what they are not.

3. *Local school- or districtwide literacy assessments should be used primarily to inform and improve instruction but also should contribute to reporting grade-level, schoolwide, and districtwide progress in literacy to the school community.* Obviously, assessments serve multiple purposes—and should do this, as will be argued again a little later—but in an attributes framework, their primary purpose is to

inform instruction. When this occurs, teachers make the best use of assessments to support children's literacy development. At the same time, assessments should serve a summative purpose, which is to inform the school community how well students are doing as a whole. One of my pet peeves is that districts so rarely report on progress toward the literacy goals that really matter to them, yet constantly publicize mandated test scores. They shouldn't be surprised, then, when the community comes to expect that all that matters are the test scores. Don't get me wrong; test scores matter and they have to be reported. But equally, districts should publicize progress toward the literacy goals that matter to them, and they can't do this unless they systematically gather the data. Further, if the same data that are gathered to inform instruction are used to report on districtwide progress toward literacy attributes, then the community will not only hear how well the district is doing on state tests but also how well it's doing toward district literacy goals. And this, in turn, will prevent the public from thinking that the only definition of literacy is what's measured by the state tests.

4. *Mandated State English/Language Arts examinations are a critical aspect of a district's literacy assessment but should not be used as sole or primary assessments of progress toward literacy attributes.* Whatever anyone thinks about mandated state or federal tests, the political consequences of ignoring them can be disastrous. I have often said to rebellious teachers that their freedom to engage students in the kinds of literacy activities they believe are essential to the growth of genuine literacy ultimately depends on how well their students do on measures they strongly oppose. Districts tend to leave teachers alone if the test scores are good and increasingly confine and micromanage them if the test scores are poor or declining. If, on the other hand, teachers separate genuine literacy from test-defined literacy (that is, what's needed to do well on a multiple-choice test) and prepare students for both types, students can actually do well on tests and become genuinely literate at the same time. The big mistake for teachers is to ignore the literacy skills needed to pass tests, and the big mistake for school districts

is to ignore the instructional contributions for achieving genuine literacy. They are typically different kinds of literacy, and students need to become good at both of them. Of course, genuine literacy pays off far more handsomely in the long run, but you may have a hard time convincing school officials, state education departments, and elected officials of this.

5. *Assessments should be economical and, wherever possible, embedded within regular classroom instruction.* E. B. White once remarked that when revising a composition, one should systematically remove words until the last one you take out completely destroys the meaning, and then put it back! I feel the same way about literacy assessment. Why test 220 sight words when 100 will yield the same results? Will 50 do? Or could we do away with sight word lists all together and assess them embedded in reading authentic text?

Recently, I conducted an exercise in a district in which teachers were asked to say what literacy assessments were used in their schools and then to align these to the literacy attributes. There were some interesting surprises. One was that some important literacy attributes weren't assessed at all (listening, speaking), but some (for example, decoding fluency) were assessed by no fewer than five measures. One of the teachers said that they'd like to assess students' listening and speaking, but (1) they didn't know how, and (2) there really wasn't enough time to do it anyway. With so many fluency measures, I'm not surprised there wasn't enough time. Reducing the number of fluency measures would not only implement the principle of economy but, more important, eliminate fluency as the major indicator of reading ability and progress. Further, it opens up the possibility of finding ways to keep track of students' progress in other areas such as speaking and listening.

Assessments should not only be economical; they need to be incorporated as much as possible into daily classroom life. This not only makes them less time-consuming; it also promotes the concept of multiple observations of literacy behaviors. A one-shot measure of a student's reading or writing performance, however standardized or normed the measure might be, is just one sample. Teachers have the opportunity across a year to sample hundreds of reading and writing performances by individual students, which gives them a far more reliable sample from which to draw conclusions about where a student is and what progress has been made.

However, putting this into practice can raise hackles, at least to begin with, and especially if there's been little or no assessment in the past. I vividly remember in a small rural school sitting across the table from a first-grade teacher, who, on learning about the assessments we were putting in place across the elementary grades, complained, "Well, I see all we'll be doing next year is assessing the kids! There won't be any instruction going on at all, so there'll be nothing to assess!" A year later, when I returned to the district with some ideas about how to simplify the assessments, this same teacher said, "I don't know why you're here; we're perfectly satisfied with our assessments, and there's no need to change any of them!" I resisted the temptation to remind her of what she'd said the previous year and instead asked about how the assessments were working out. At first, the district had hired aides to allow the classroom teachers to administer DRAs three times a year. By the end of the year, however, the teachers had incorporated not only the DRAs into their regular classroom routines but all the other literacy attribute assessments as well. Apparently, there was enough time for teaching after all!

The challenge of embedding literacy assessment into daily classroom routines seems to be more pronounced in the upper-elementary grades and especially in secondary schools, where assessment is often thought of as tests that are separate from the curriculum. The reason for this, I believe, is that the further up the grade levels a student progresses, the more traditional the grading becomes, and in order to have grades, teachers usually insist on *tests*. Larger class loads also contribute to this. It becomes much harder to observe and record multiple instances of students' literacy behaviors when you have responsibility for over one hundred students, as opposed to twenty-five.

6. *Assessments should draw on observations, conversations, and analysis of samples of literacy behaviors, not just literacy tasks or tests.* This is probably one of the most important principles. It is sad that so much of what professional teachers know about their students is discounted or thought to be "subjective," while "objective" measures are given credence far beyond their capabilities. It isn't so much that I oppose standardized, normed literacy assessments; rather, that what teachers observe, talk with their students about, or analyze from multiple samples of student work provides such rich and valid information about where students are in their literacy development. Formal measures play an important role, too, but they should always be used in conjunction with the other forms of evidence of students' literacy status and growth.

Observations are particularly appropriate for gathering evidence of the process of students' literacy learning. It is very difficult, for example, to make sense of most kindergartners' writing unless you observe them while they are composing. If you did, you'd learn that Sarah's drawing of a giraffe in her apple orchard was "borrowed" from Daniel's account of the trip his family took to the zoo. You might also hear a child rehearsing what he intends to write or speaking the words as they are scribbled down in what's called linear mock writing (unintelligible squiggles that look wordlike but contain no letters).

Some literacy activities have to be observed if they are to be kept track of. Teachers won't be able to say how proficient their students are in speaking, listening, and viewing unless they actually observe students engaged in these behaviors. As students represent what they know and are learning, much of it results in samples that can be analyzed (for example, drawings, writing), but much is ephemeral and has to be observed while it's occurring. Playing (with blocks, in the dramatic play center or in free-choice time) serves as a critical contributor to literacy development. But unless the teacher observes or records these activities, they leave no tangible evidence behind. In fact, I've seen teachers periodically videotape students engaged in dramatic play and photograph their block creations, just for the purpose of assessing their status and growth in these literacy contributions.

Unlike observations, conversations involve active participation and interaction between teachers and students. This in turn makes it possible for teachers to find out what students know and are learning and to probe with questions. Book and writing conferences are forms of conversations, as are literature circles, and in skilled hands, serve both as learning and assessment tools. This is demonstrated by Peterson and Eeds (1990) in a book aptly titled *Grand Conversations*. In their approach, teachers listen to students' understandings of the books they are reading and then challenge them to dig deeper into multiple layers of meaning. Teachers cannot fail to comprehend the depth of students' literary understanding through these conversations, while simultaneously deepening the students' understanding.

Conversations can take place with individual students, small groups, and the whole class; over time, each provides different but immensely useful evidence of progress toward many of the attributes.

7. *Formal literacy assessments should have best available reliability and validity.* In the current assessment environment, prescribed by No Child Left Behind legislation, only "scientific," "evidence-based" measures of literacy achievement are sanctioned, and school districts have been increasingly reluctant to use any assessment that doesn't have rigorous psychometric properties. In the past three years, I have advocated keeping track of what's important, even if the measures for doing so aren't psychometrically perfect. The question is, which is worse—psychometrically valid measures of trivial or incomplete aspects of literacy or informal and possibly psychometrically shaky measures of important aspects of literacy? Both have issues of reliability, validity, and representativeness. I think we need the best assessments we can find that tell us where our students are, relative to our expectations, and this will inevitably mean mixing formal and informal measures—valid and reliable measures of decoding alongside reading logs; informal

assessments of comprehending big ideas alongside standardized measures of literal comprehension. Acknowledging the imperfections of all assessments is important, but this should not deter us from doing our best to say where each student is, relative to the literacy attributes, so we can redouble our efforts to support students' progress toward them.

Use of the Principles in Practice

We need to think hard about how often to assess students and how best we can integrate assessment with instruction. We also need to use a variety of measures (observation, conversation, formal and informal tasks, analysis of samples) to track students' progress and status. Keeping assessments simple, unobtrusive, yet comprehensive and as valid as we can possibly make them is the key here.

Although I've laid out these major sources of evidence for literacy learning one-by-one, in real life, they tend to work together. Try this experiment. Ask a teacher to pick a student in his or her class. Then ask whether this student reads widely. Suppose the teacher answers yes. Then ask, "Tell me how you know this. What evidence would you provide to back up your judgment?" In almost all cases, there'll be evidence from *observations* ("I see Matthew reading all the time," or "I never see Lauretta with a book"), from *conversations* ("Sally can't wait to chat to me about the book she's reading," or "I can't talk with Paul about what he's reading, because he's never reading"), or from *analysis of samples* ("Take a look at Fred's reading log; it's obvious that he's reading both fiction and nonfiction, even poetry but not nearly as much," or "Deidre's log shows that she's a voracious reader of poetry, but I'm struggling to get her to read more nonfiction."). Could the teacher be wrong about these students' reading habits? Possibly, if the independent reading in class was linked to rewards (for example, Book-It), and if the teacher didn't really know or care about what the students were reading. But if the assessments were triangulated—in other words, teachers had conversations with students about the books they read or asked students to reflect on their reading in journals and didn't rely solely on reading logs—it's unlikely they would be misinformed. But it does happen. I did a study (Walmsley, Rosenthal et al. 1996) in which we tracked the independent reading of ten students from fifth to seventh grade. We learned that some students read voraciously on their own but wouldn't share that reading with a teacher, either because they wanted to keep it private (one student told us he didn't want his reading on the Civil War to become part of the class activities) or because they didn't think it was anything the teacher would be interested in.

More recently, I was introduced to a fifth-grader who had read more books than anyone else in a school that used *Accelerated Reader*; she confessed to me—only after I promised her I wouldn't tell her teachers—that she didn't really read many books at all; she used various ploys (for example, selecting books with movie versions she'd seen, consulting Cliffs Notes) to accumulate the points needed to "win." This is a situation where it might be wise not to rely solely on the *Accelerated Reader* log.

These accounts certainly reinforce the difficulties of creating and employing valid assessments of the amount and breadth of students' reading. But if done sensibly and economically, it is possible to provide evidence to support a judgment that a student is reading a lot and reading widely. More important, if that's a literacy goal, it *has* to be kept track of. Otherwise, it will be accomplished by students for whom it comes naturally and not by students for whom it doesn't. Unmeasured or unrecorded, it probably won't last long as a goal, either.

What goes for keeping track of "reading widely" also goes for all aspects of language arts. Although each area calls for different kinds of assessments, the moment we say that an area is too hard to measure, or the assessments are too subjective, or we don't have time to assess it, that area becomes less important as a goal and, over the long run, diminishes in importance as a goal. However, once a district commits itself to keeping track of students' progress across all the important literacy goals, ways will be found to assess them, and over time, these assessments will improve in both validity and reliability and will become easier to assess and to embed into regular classroom instruction.

Summary

Keeping track of students' progress towards each of the literacy attributes is a critical component of the framework. For each literacy attribute, teachers and administrators need to know where students are and to have confidence that the assessments provide valid information. The challenge is treading that thin line between gathering useful data and overdoing literacy assessments, especially at a time when state and federal assessments have grown exponentially in frequency and consequences.

If they hold firm to the principles outlined in this chapter, especially embedding assessment into the daily routines of classrooms and keeping assessments to a minimum, teachers can keep track of students' progress toward the attributes, and they'll find the information invaluable for planning and revising instructional techniques.

Of course, keeping track of students' progress and accomplishments in language arts is one thing. Reporting to parents is another, because report cards have to say how well or poorly a student is doing, and that requires developing scoring criteria and determining levels of performance. The challenge of reporting student progress in language arts is the subject of the next chapter.

7

REPORTING LITERACY PROGRESS

In Chapter Six, I discussed the challenge of keeping track of students' progress in an attributes framework. Of course, a major reason to assess student progress is to provide the evidence for completing report cards, to share with parents how well their children are doing.

In this chapter, I want to focus on reporting literacy progress. I'll start with my concerns about report cards at both the elementary and secondary levels and then describe some ways they might be revised to fit within an attributes framework.

The Problem with Report Cards

If there is one thing I can generally predict, especially in elementary schools, it's that the language arts section of the report cards doesn't align with the language arts curriculum. If you're an elementary teacher or administrator reading this, take a minute and pull out a copy of your report card. Does it have *reading* and *writing* as headers—but not *listening* and *speaking* (I wouldn't expect it to have *viewing* and *representing*, given they are rarely thought of as part of language arts)? How well does it represent the school's or district's language arts goals?

I've studied school report cards for a long time and have some thoughts about why they so frequently misrepresent or underrepresent important language arts goals. First, there's a problem in the way that report cards are generally created. Typically, one committee designs the language arts curriculum while another does the report card, not necessarily on the same timetable, so that a report card committee might work on the report card one year, only to have the language arts curriculum reworked the following year. If they are to connect, they need to be worked on together. Another problem is that teachers don't heed E. B. White's advice about brevity. For whatever reason, suggestions for what to include on the report card tend to get added rather than synthesized, so report cards have a tendency to include more rather than less. This is especially true when it comes to the perennial favorite topic of a report card, namely behaviors. Just how many ways do we need to say that the student is cooperative, pays attention, and does what he or she is told? Apparently, many!

Another issue is that old habits die hard. Ever wondered why so many elementary report cards list *reading*, *writing*, and *spelling* as their major headings? (Or even *reading*, *writing*, *handwriting*, *spelling*, and *grammar*?) It's probably because these were the "subjects" of a traditional language arts program, stretching back to the beginning of the twentieth century. Yet shouldn't *handwriting*, *spelling*, and even *grammar* be incorporated into writing, rather than being listed as separate and equal to it? It isn't that these are unimportant aspects of language arts; rather, they shouldn't be raised to the same level as reading and writing. Also, traditional definitions of language arts shied away from *listening* and *speaking* and uniformly ignored *viewing* and *representing*, so it's a rare event to see these as categories on report cards. However, many school districts I observe or work with do have listening and speaking as important goals, yet they are nowhere to be seen on the report cards. And if they are, *listening* is defined almost exclusively as a behavior (for example, "pays attention in class") rather than a cognitive activity (for example, "understands what is heard").

In middle and high schools, language arts morphs into English. English report cards typically have a single grade (sometimes with pithy computer-generated comments) that captures in a letter or number the student's academic performance, as well as effort in the class. It is very hard to unpack this grade and determine whether the student can, for example, read with understanding, or communicate effectively in writing, or has read widely. In fact, a student who can do all these things very well but has failed to hand in assignments could easily get a poorer grade than a less able student who has completed all the work. But to be fair, with classes of over one hundred students, generating report cards with the same detail as elementary teachers routinely offer is not realistic.

As I see it, elementary report cards suffer from some systemic maladies. They generally aren't well aligned with the language arts goals and curriculum. They over-represent traditional aspects of language arts (reading, spelling, and so on) and under-represent others (especially listening and speaking but also viewing and representing). They overdo reporting of behaviors. And they often poorly represent aspects of literacy within categories—for example, detailing decoding skills, while ignoring anything but low-level comprehension skills. Finally, they tend to report on too much. It's a dead giveaway when you open up a report card for first grade that's 8½ X 14 inches, with 6-point fonts throughout!

Over the past few years, I have begun to realize that a fresh approach is called for in the design of report cards, at both the elementary and secondary levels. Although there are still many unresolved challenges, I'd like to identify the main issues and propose some strategies for addressing them.

What Report Cards Should Report On

The issue here is whether report cards should say where students are, relative to our expectations of where they should be, or how well they are doing, relative to the instruction we are providing. A good example is spelling. Should a report card say that a student spells words correctly in his written compositions or report on how well he has performed on spelling tests based on the spelling program? In the first instance, the primary definition of a student "doing well" in spelling comes from examining how well he spells in the real world of writing. In the second, it's all about how well he is doing in the curriculum. My experience is that most elementary teachers prefer the report card to communicate the latter. Frequently, when working on report cards, teachers will say, "We can't report on whether a child decodes well until we've taught it," even though there are many children who already decode well prior to instruction in decoding. So they delay assessing decoding until, say, the middle of first grade. In turn, this provides inaccurate information about how well first-graders are decoding, because the ones who already decode well aren't being assessed until a later point.

This also comes into play when I recommend starting to use the DRA at the beginning of kindergarten, to get a good picture of the decoding levels of all the children as they enter. In most instances, I'm told that not enough children read well enough yet to make this a viable proposition. In other words, we haven't progressed far enough into the kindergarten curriculum, so starting the DRA in, say, January, is a better idea. I counter that if one of our attributes is "reads fluently," then knowing how even beginning kindergartners do this is valuable and necessary to know. Since the DRA stretches down to the very beginnings of decoding fluency, administering this to a beginning kindergartner makes sense (with, obviously, some exceptions). We have a benchmark to start the year off and can say that "X" percent of this year's kindergartners are at this level in one aspect of reading fluency. What we do with this information, of course, is a different matter. I assume that we will use it carefully to provide children with the most appropriate experiences and instruction to help them move along toward, in this case, reading fluency. However, I'm well aware that if the information is not used properly, it might have been better not to have gathered it at all. My experience is that teachers generally act more appropriately with good information, when they have good information.

Reporting Effort Versus Accomplishment

The second issue is about effort versus accomplishment. Of course, the two are connected in some major ways. But when it comes to the report card, they often get very muddled—especially so with struggling students. Should a report card take into account the level of effort a student is expending when reporting on reading or writing "levels"? The moment you do this, you can no longer say with any precision where the student is, relative to literacy goals. Or, rather, you redefine the goals for each student. Thus saying that a student who barely can decode words in a simple story is "reading fluently" conveys the message that his or her fluency is good, when what it actually means is that he or she is making good progress in reading fluency, despite not being able to read fluently by any standard definition. This is like reporting one's weight in terms of the effort being expended on dieting or in terms of losing a pound or so, while ignoring the actual weight itself. I would argue that effort and progress within a curriculum are important contributions to outcomes (and should be recognized as such), but the report card's primary function should be to say where the child is, relative to the expectations for all children. In other words, report the actual "weight" and keep this separate from the effort and curriculum progress. Don't lump them both together!

In schools I have been working with, we have put this principle to the test and, surprisingly, the place where it has succeeded best has been with struggling students. Parents of these children know full well that their children struggle but are often only given the "good news" about effort and progress within a curriculum with lowered expectations, so they really don't know how their child is doing relative to the different aspects of literacy. A report card that provides them with information about how well their child reads fluently, or reads widely, or uses effective language and style gives them details of where their child is, relative to a school's expectations. One parent told me, "This is the first time the school is telling me the truth about my child's language abilities, and I appreciate their frankness. I also notice that my child has strengths in areas I never knew about or appreciated—like viewing and representing."

Anchoring Expectations

In both of the issues described, you'll notice that I've used the term *knowing where a student is, relative to the attributes or expectations,* without actually defining what that means. Let me start this explanation with a story. At the height of the Whole Language era, when portfolio assessment was very popular, I bumped into a teacher in Idaho, who had transformed her teacher-parent conferences into sessions where she laid out to the parent all the language arts artifacts their child had produced over the last marking period and proceeded to walk the parents through them to show what the child had accomplished. She noticed that one particular couple sat there with a pained expression on their faces, getting more troubled as the demonstration wore on. Finally, the mother interrupted her: "So, what you're telling me is that my child isn't doing well; otherwise you would have said what grade level she's reading at, right?" Actually, the child was reading well. The parents had completely missed the point of the exercise! After that, the teacher began each parent conference with the statement, "Your child is reading at 3.6 (or whatever) grade level," and then she'd proceed to the portfolio. No one complained after that.

The point here is that a literacy expectation or attribute has to be "pegged" in some way to what teachers think a child should be doing at this age, or grade level. What the Idaho parents needed was this anchor point, something they could relate to that said their child was at or above or below an expectation for that grade level. Even though neither they nor the teacher really knew what "reading at 3.6 grade level" meant in real-world terms, it provided the peg onto which everything else could hang. No amount of laying out of artifacts could substitute for this, even though the information in this demonstration was enormously more descriptive of what their child could actually do. It took me a long time to figure this out, and it isn't only parents who need an anchor; it's teachers, too.

Over a lengthy period of trial and error—mostly the latter—I think I have arrived at an approach that is gaining traction in the schools I work with. Basically, it defines an expectation in terms of what we would expect a "solid" student to be able to demonstrate in a given grade level. In other words, not the "average" level of performance—that's too low—but what, over time, we would expect of a student performing well in a given attribute. In receptive literacy areas like reading, this can be operationalized in terms of a student's ability to make sense (understand the main ideas, even the big ideas) of particular fiction and nonfiction books and other material used in the grade level. In my most recent project, we have co-opted Fountas and Pinnell's "levels" to provide clear guidelines for what would constitute a student's level of decoding fluency, so that we can peg their fluency to a book of a particular level. On the expressive side, the provision of exemplars of writing can serve the same function, although it turns out that matching a student's piece of writing to someone else's exemplar is not as easy as it sounds. And it inevitably leads to creating writing tasks based on specific assignments to get a better fit between the exemplars and the students' performance—a practice that makes it easier to compare but restricts the writing samples too much. Similarly, we can use videotaped exemplars of students speaking to "anchor" various aspects of this attribute.

I want to caution against trying to arrive at too precise a definition of *levels of performance*, because even in the case of leveled books or written or spoken exemplars, there is enough variation to give pause to the idea that any aspect of literacy can be truly "pegged." It's funny, isn't it, that we can all recognize and understand what is meant by a "good" reader, but defining that in precise, concrete terms is very difficult indeed, because it involves defining what *reading* means, as well as taking the reader's age or stage of development into consideration. Yet if we don't strive for some level of precision, teachers and administrators are likely to say that the whole exercise is too subjective. Strange that saying a child reads at 3.6 grade level is considered objective, whereas saying that the same child has a good understanding of *Tuck Everlasting* is thought to be too subjective!

Rather than trying to define what it means to meet a literacy expectation primarily through articulating characteristics of texts, may I suggest also repeated, collaborative conversations among professionals within and between grade levels, using a range of student examples across the language arts. These conversations will capture more of the complexities and variations than is possible in specific tasks or even rubrics. Used in conjunction with rubrics, they will increase the consistency of observations and analyses of samples, as well as contribute significantly to consensus on what it means, in a given grade level, that a student meets, exceeds, or falls short of expectations in a literacy attribute.

The Challenge of Middle and High School Report Cards

Finally, we have to grapple with the challenge of reporting students' progress in middle and high school. In my work with districts pre-K through grade 12, there is rarely any disagreement on articulating literacy attributes across the grades, in fact quite the contrary. Middle and high school educators are delighted to participate in an exercise that provides a common set of literacy expectations, pre-K through grade 12, especially when they see that the attributes represent the literary, not just literacy, expectations they have of students, and particularly that the instructional contributions in the elementary schools lay the groundwork for what's expected in the upper grades. (I don't have to explain *big ideas* to high school English teachers but sometimes struggle with it with teachers in the early grades.) But when the attention turns to assessment and reporting, middle and high school teachers start to twitch. I can see why. With a teaching load of 100 to 150 students and significant amounts of homework to correct, the prospect of adding to what they already see as an oppressive amount of assessment is more than daunting. Secondary teachers have a reputation for saying no to reforms that involve an increase in workload, and in most of the projects I've done in middle and high school, they've ended up doing just that. Interestingly, no one has challenged the logic behind an attributes approach—that we articulate literacy expectations, we agree on non-negotiable instructional contributions, and we keep track of students' progress toward them—but they balk at actually keeping track of and reporting where students are, with respect to the attributes.

Part of the challenge is that there is already in place an assessment and reporting regimen that is seriously at odds with an attributes framework. English is taught as a separate subject area, with assignments and tests that contribute points to a single letter or numerical grade. Of course, this aligns with the grading system used in colleges and is a vital component of the process of applying for college. These grades are the sine qua non of assessment in high school, and you challenge them at your peril.

In some of my early projects, I was foolish enough to try to change this tradition, arguing that what was good for the elementary grades (attributes-instruction, contributions-assessment-report cards) was also good for middle and high school. It didn't work, not because teachers weren't willing to try it but because any system that couldn't produce GPAs, involved additional work, and couldn't fit into the existing report cards and interim reports was unacceptable.

Once I had accepted the reality of the traditional grading system, I started to think about how to make literacy attribute assessment work in a middle and high school environment. As luck would have it, at about the same time, my own department at the University at Albany was embarking on an assessment journey of its own—seeking accreditation for the first time. The Teacher Education Accreditation Council (TEAC), the accreditation agency, set us a challenge that looked remarkably similar to the one I used in schools. We were asked to articulate our goals for students graduating from our master's programs, to align our instructional sequence with these goals, and to provide evidence that our students achieved what we claimed for them—in essence, an attributes approach! As I struggled with my university colleagues to shift our paradigm, I noticed exactly the same reaction by them as I had already seen in middle and high schools. Like high school teachers, we teach our curriculum through courses, we both use written and oral assignments that take significant amounts of time to correct, and we both use single-letter or numerical grades to evaluate each student's progress toward completion of their program.

Unlike high schools, however, our master's programs don't lead to a final examination or thesis, so we've had a much harder time aligning the content of our courses (the instructional contributions) to our expectations, because prior to the accreditation process, we never seriously articulated what we wanted our graduate students to look like as they completed their studies. In the end, we created for our literacy certification programs a clear set of expectations (attributes), showed how each course contributed to one or more of these expectations, and then spent an enormous amount of time debating how best to assess each student's progress. I knew this was going to be contentious, and it was. All the same arguments as the middle and high school teachers made were now repeated—too much assessment, why can't we just use grades, it interferes with our academic freedom, there's too much record keeping, and so on. In the end, we agreed that our assessment would comprise several elements. For example, careful monitoring of the fit between each course syllabus and the required content would be required, so that although instructors could exercise academic freedom in the selection of reading material, assignments, and the course pedagogy, they had to cover specific topics and had to create assessments for those learning outcomes that contributed to the department's goals for each student. And for each of these assessments, the student work had to be submitted to the department. Our "report cards" haven't changed (students still get the traditional academic transcript), but the evidence supporting the grades has been transformed.

We must have done something right, because after the external audit, TEAC granted us the full five-year provisional accreditation and has used our approach as a model for other universities to follow. But what this exercise taught me was that if one figured out a way to navigate a path between traditional assessment routines and new reporting requirements, a fairly satisfactory compromise could be reached. Now in our second year of a new approach, what some of us thought would be completely overwhelming is now pretty standard practice, and no one is complaining about the additional workload.

Back to middle and high school: after I abandoned imposing an elementary-type report card on secondary teachers, I tried several approaches. Let me describe each of them briefly.

Rethinking the Grade Book

With some young, energetic teachers in a brand-new high school, we tried to change the grade books used by English teachers so they aligned with the attributes, rather than simply with a grade-point average. The idea here was that if we could alter the way teachers gathered the evidence of students' learning, they would have less difficulty reporting on them. So if the grade book had attributes as categories, with assignments aligned to these, then students would get grades in the traditional way, but these could also be analyzed by attribute. Although this approach eventually failed, what it did was show how to integrate attributes into both the content of the English courses and the assessments. In fact, in several other districts, aligning the attributes to the course content through mapping exercises proved to be extremely valuable, and teachers enthusiastically embraced it. In fact, the only difficulty I have faced with this is districts insisting on curriculum mapping at the same time, using a completely different framework, and thoroughly confusing the teaching staff.

Linking Attributes to Report Cards

When I was a high school student in England, my report cards were simply a collection of loose-leaf pages of narratives, bound together.

When my own children went to middle and high school, their report cards were much more mechanical, comprising numerical grades, accompanied by one or two computer-generated phrases like "Is A Pleasure to Have in Class" (for my daughter), and "Does Not Complete Assignments in a Timely Fashion" (for my son). This format is typically the one used for secondary report cards in the schools I've been working with.

What we developed in one middle school in downstate New York was to retain the traditional English grades but create an additional list of comments for teachers to use that were based on the attributes. So a teacher could assign a grade in the usual way but then select one of the attribute comments to go along with it. Thus, a student could receive an A-minus in an English course but underneath might be a computer-generated comment saying "Does not read widely" or "Has difficulty with basic reading fluency," or "Communicates idea effectively in writing." We immediately ran into technical difficulties. Phrases had character limits imposed by the computer software, so only two comments were allowed per subject, and given how little could be communicated, teachers generally picked comments that were either highly positive or highly negative. In other words, this technique prevents any kind of balanced reporting across attributes. However, given the constraints under which we were working, nothing else was possible, and the middle school continues using this approach. You can see how this looks in Exhibit 7.1.

Linking Attributes to the Interim Report Card

Secondary schools issue interim report cards that have a much more flexible format, allowing comments to be made by teachers, so I've focused on these as a possible approach to reporting on student progress toward the attributes. One barrier is that interims are typically used to flag only those students having difficulties with learning, so using them to report all students' progress is quite a challenge.

Exhibit 7.1. Middle School List of Comments.

Attribute Category	Old/New	#	Comment
Listening	New	L001	Critical-responsive listener/4
Listening	New	L002	Critical-responsive listener/3
Listening	New	L003	Critical-responsive listener/2
Listening	New	L004	Critical-responsive listener/1
Reading	New	R001	Understands what is read/4
Reading	New	R002	Understands what is read/3
Reading	New	R003	Understands what is read/2
Reading	New	R004	Understands what is read/1
Reading	New	R005	Has extensive reading vocab
Reading	New	R006	Reading vocab shows growth
Reading	New	R007	Has minimal reading vocab
Reading	New	R008	Does not read enough
Reading	New	R009	Only reads simple books
Reading	New	R010	Reads very widely
Reading	New	R011	Reads widely
Reading	New	R012	Does not read widely
Reading	New	R013	Understands big ideas/4
Reading	New	R014	Understands big ideas/3
Reading	New	R015	Understands big ideas/2
Reading	New	R016	Understands big ideas/1
Reading	New	R017	Uses reading strategies/4

Nonetheless, using the interim for this purpose is gaining some traction. In order for it to work, however, the attributes themselves have to be embedded into the curriculum, and teachers have to be comfortable with the instructional contributions. Once that is in place, they are much more willing and supportive of the idea that reporting this information is worth the effort.

The interim itself can be quite simple: just list the attributes and have teachers indicate student progress toward each of them. The first attempt at this was to list each attribute and then have teachers "score" them on a 6-point scale. (In New York elementary schools, there's a 4-point scale; beyond eighth grade, a 6-point scale is used). This was too cumbersome. I then created a "slider" from 1 to 6 so that a teacher could simply indicate with a dot on the slider to indicate the student's performance. This worked much better—it was designed to be filled out on a computer to ease data entry and let the computer generate the interim—but in the end, wasn't adopted by the district. Exhibit 7.2 shows what this design looks like.

More recently, I have been experimenting with a similar format but a simpler method of reporting—either a 1 to 4 "grade" or a check box against each attribute, where the teacher simply provides a double check (√√) to indicate that the student exceeds grade-level expectations, a single check (√) to indicate meeting the expectations, a minus (−) to indicate falling below expectations, and a double minus (−−) to indicate falling far below expectations. Obviously, this reporting system cannot be reliable or valid unless there is evidence sitting behind the check marks, but before this assessment becomes standard practice, there is significant professional development on the attributes and the instructional contributions, so the evidence sits closely behind the check marks. Also, in the middle and high school, these interims would only be completed twice a year. Other interims would remain as a mechanism for flagging students with learning and other issues. Of course, the attribute interims perform the same function and with much greater specificity.

One version of this, as shown in Exhibit 7.3, was designed for use in a school district in the Catskills, New York. It's an interesting mixture of traditional grading and attribute reporting.

Another version, as shown in Exhibit 7.4, is a proposed high school interim, using just the literacy attributes.

Although these attribute assessments haven't been employed on anything like the scale of the elementary report cards, I am hopeful that at last we have found a way to continue reporting student status and progress toward the literacy attributes beyond

Exhibit 7.2. High School Slider Interim.

	Marking Period								Marking Period							Comments:
Level:	1	2	3	4	5	6			1	2	3	4	5	6	

Reading
Reads widely

Reads for Understanding
- *reads fluently*
- *reads expressively*
- *reads deeply*
- *reads for information*
- *responds to text (literary, personal)*
- *has an extensive reading vocabulary*

Writing
Communicates ideas effectively
Demonstrates effective language/style
Uses correct and appropriate mechanics
- *spelling*
- *grammar*
- *punctuation/capitalization*
- *presentation*

Listening
Understands what is heard, is a critical listener

Speaking
Communicates ideas, uses appropriate techniques

Viewing
Understands what is observed, is a critical viewer

Representing
Can represent what is known in a variety of media

Exhibit 7.3. High School Interim.

English Language Arts Report Card

Name_____   Date_____

Expressive Language

Grade Scale:
4 = exceeds expectations   3 = performs at grade level
2 = performs below grade   1 = requires significant
    level   remediation

**Assessment of Student's Written   Grade
Expression**

Meaning (Ideas): How well student's
   responses
show understanding and interpretation of tasks   _____
fulfill purpose and requirements
   of the task   _____

Development: How well student's ideas are
   elaborated with details
uses several details to support thesis statement   _____
uses relevant and accurate details   _____

Organization: How well student's response
   is organized
pre-writing planning is evident   _____
introduction clearly states thesis of essay,
   gets reader's attention   _____
each body paragraph focuses on a main idea
   with specific details   _____
ideas are in logical order that makes sense
   to reader (response
   has a clear beginning, middle, and end)   _____
transitional words or phrases show   _____
   relationships among ideas

conclusion summarizes or restates main ideas,
  gives sense of closure   _____

Language Use: How well student
  effectively uses words and sentence structure
  (voice, word choice, sentence fluency)

uses vivid language with a sense of energy,
  appropriate to audience   _____

uses precise, sophisticated vocabulary that
  clarifies ideas   _____

uses fluent, expressive sentences that are
  easy to read   _____

varies sentence structure (some long, some
  short sentences)   _____

Conventions: How well student has mastered
  mechanics of writing

grammar and usage(contains few, if any,
  minor errors)   _____

spelling (contains few, if any, minor errors)   _____

capitalization (contains few, if any,
  minor errors)   _____

punctuation (contains few, if any,
  minor errors)   _____

paragraphing (indents to show start of
  each new topic)   _____

complete sentences (contains no sentence
  fragments or run-ons)   _____

Assessment of Student's Speaking

Communicates ideas effectively,
  using appropriate techniques   _____

Assessment of Student's Representation of Concepts

Communicates ideas effectively, using
  appropriate media and techniques   _____

Receptive Language

Assessment of Student's Reading

Reads Fluently (is able to decode
and use appropriate reading strategies to
read smoothly; at a pace appropriate
to grade-level text, as determined
by reading aloud or with teacher) _____

Comprehends what is read (uses
appropriate reading strategies to
make sense of text; demonstrates
comprehension on tests) _____

Reads widely (from a variety of genres
including novels, short stories, drama,
poetry, nonfiction, etc.; based on
reading logs, literature tests) _____

Reads substantially (minimum of
200 pages on grade level per quarter,
more if reading below
grade level) _____

Assessment of Student's Listening

Is critical and responsive listener _____

Assessment of Student's Viewing

Is critical and responsive viewer _____

elementary school, yet place no significant additional burden on
middle and high school teachers with their large student enroll-
ment. However, until these become standard practice in the
schools that have adopted an attribute approach, I can't guarantee
that the problem has been completely solved.

Exhibit 7.4. High School Attributes-Based Interim.

Literacy Attributes Interim Report

Student Name_____   Semester/Year_____

READING
__Decodes fluently
__Reads expressively
__Understands
   informational texts
__Understands literary
   texts
__Understands "big idea"
__Has an extensive reading
   vocabulary
__Reads widely

LISTENING
__Is a critical and responsive
   listener

WRITING
__Communicates ideas
   effectively
__Develops and organizes
   writing
__Uses effective language/
   style
__Uses correct/ appropriate
   mechanics

SPEAKING
__Communicates ideas
   effectively

REPRESENTING
__Communicates ideas
   effectively in a variety of
   media

VIEWING
__Is a critical and responsive viewer

COMMENTS

KNOWLEDGE OF THE WORLD
__Has extensive background knowledge

Key
√√ = exceeds grade-level expectations
 √ = meets grade-level expectations
 — = falls short of grade-level expectations
— — = is significantly below grade-level expectations

Redesigning Report Cards

Redesigning report cards at the elementary level seems to be an endless process for school districts, often taking several years and numerous committee meetings. Middle and high schools don't change theirs nearly so often, and even when they do, it's typically to accommodate a switch to new computer software.

For me, designing an elementary or secondary report card in an attributes framework is both simple and relatively quick, because most of the preparation is already done. For example, no one has to agonize over what gets to be included in language arts (it's already articulated—the headers are Reading, Writing, Speaking, Listening, Viewing, and Representing), and no one has to argue about what sits underneath them (it's the attributes themselves). So the vast majority of the work typically undertaken by a report card committee has already been done, and what's more, it is already completely aligned with the district's language arts expectations (attributes) and the curriculum (instructional contributions).

But there is work to be done. Usually, what I have to convince a district to do first is to agree to revise all the report cards, even if they've recently changed them. In one district, my efforts to do this were less compelling than the report card committee that had just completely overhauled the kindergarten report card. The problem was that the district had already invested heavily in an attributes approach that included the kindergarten program, but they felt that noses would be put out of joint if they asked the kindergarten programs to abandon what they had just completed. Given what ensued, they should have bitten the bullet, because we now had a kindergarten curriculum that was undergoing significant changes toward an attributes approach, yet a report card that clung to a traditional "readiness" philosophy that the district was desperately trying to change. My protestations notwithstanding, the kindergartens adhered to their readiness approach, largely because they had a report card that matched it, causing huge consternation both among teachers and administrators. In the end, we did change the kindergarten report card, but in hindsight it would have been better to grin and bear the initial angst and move on. I am working now in a district that has also recently made significant changes to its elementary report cards, but in this situation, I don't have to make the case for switching to a new format, thank goodness.

The other issue we have to address is that very rarely will a school district reform its language arts programs on the same schedule as other areas, so we face the prospect of changing not the whole report card but just the language arts section. This generally is not problematic, given that most report cards separate the various subject areas, but it does cause difficulties if the scoring criteria are different for language arts than other areas. Many districts strive for a consistent scoring rubric for the entire report card, but that's not likely to work for an attributes-driven language arts report card section. Further, complications may arise if the existing report card uses a combination of grades and "scores," but the language arts section only uses scores. But the biggest challenge by far will be persuading the teaching staff to think differently about what the report card is reporting—achievement pegged to grade-level expectations or achievement and progress intermingled with effort. For the purposes of this discussion, I'm going to assume that bridge has been crossed and will focus solely on the design of the report card itself.

Finally, although all the examples that follow are similar in design, an attributes framework doesn't insist on a specific report card format. I wish I had been able to work in a school district that uses a narrative report card, because it would be easy to adapt that to attributes.

Before and After

Perhaps the best way to illustrate the difference between a traditional and an attributes report card is to share an example of a report card before and after the transition to an attributes framework. Here in Exhibit 7.5 is a previous one, from Gilbertsville-Mt. Upton:

Exhibit 7.5. Original GMU Report Card.

Marking System

A Excellent   * observed frequently
B Good   + observed occasionally
C Fair   / not observed
D Poor
F Not Passing

	Quarters			
	1st	2nd	3rd	4th
Math				
Knows addition facts				
Knows subtraction facts				
Solves word problems				
Works accurately				
Additional skills _____				
_____				
_____				
_____				
Language Arts				
Penmanship				
Forms letters correctly				
Writes legibly				
Reading				
Reading on grade level				
Makes appropriate reading choices				
Uses appropriate word attack skills				
Applies reading strategies				
Reads fluently with expression				
Shows an interest in reading				
Writing				
Expresses ideas clearly				
Actively uses skills learned in writing				
Spelling				
Does well on weekly spelling tests				
Applies spelling skills to daily work				
Listening and Speaking				
Listens when others are speaking				
Is able to express self orally				
Contributes appropriately in group discussions				

	Quarters			
	1st	2nd	3rd	4th

Social Studies
Uses critical thinking skills to understand
cause and effect
Demonstrates understanding of new facts or
concepts
a) through class discussion
b) through projects

Science
Questions and investigates
Demonstrates understanding of new facts or
concepts
a) through class discussion
b) through projects

Social Development and Work Habits
Listens to and follows directions
Uses time wisely
Works well independently
Works well in a group
Takes pride in work
Respects property of others
Is respectful to adults
Friendly attitude toward classmates
Accepts responsibility
Accepts suggestions

Attendance
Days absent
Days tardy

And here in Exhibit 7.6 is the revised report card, with its literacy attributes aligned:

Exhibit 7.6. Current GMU Report Card.

		Quarters			
Reading		1	2	3	4
Decodes Fluently	*Decoding level*				
	Applies appropriate reading strategies				
	Knows conventions of print				
	Identifies letters of the alphabet				
	Identifies sound-symbol relationships				
	Knows sight words				
Understands what	*Understands informational text*				
is read	*Understands literary text*				
independently	*Understands big ideas*				
	Understands meanings of words				
	Applies appropriate comprehension strategies				
Reads Expressively					
Reads Independently					
Listening					
Is a critical and responsive listener					
Viewing					
Is a critical and responsive viewer					
Writing					
Communicates ideas effectively	*informational*				
Demonstrates effective language/style	*expressive*				
Organizes and fully develops writing					
Uses correct mechanics	*spelling*				
	grammar				
	punctuation/capitalization				
	presentation/handwriting				
Speaking					
Communicates ideas effectively in speaking, uses appropriate techniques					
Representing					
Can represent ideas through a variety of media					

Attributes	4	Exceeds grade-level expectations
	3	Meets grade-level expectations
	2	Falls below grade-level expectations
	1	Is significantly below grade-level expectations

	Quarters			
Mathematics	1	2	3	4
Applies knowledge of basic math facts				
Computes accurately				
Uses problem-solving strategies				
Understands mathematical concepts				
Additional skills				

Social Studies				
Understands cause and effect				
Understands new facts or concepts				
Contributes to class discussion				

Science				
Questions and investigates				
Understands new facts or concepts				
Contributes to class discussion				
Transference of knowledge is evident				

Work Habits				
Is well organized				
Participates in class				
Works independently				
Cooperates in groups				
Completes class assignments on time				
Completes homework assignments on time				
Respects others and property				
Takes responsibility				
Overall Effort				

Attendance				
Days absent				
Days tardy				

Summary

It is hard to underestimate the role that report cards play in defining what counts as literacy and what gets attention in the language arts curriculum. So, if the report card is not aligned with a district's literacy expectations and curriculum, it creates an alternate set of expectations. Unfortunately, this is very common, given how report cards are often created independently of the expectations and curriculum.

In an attributes framework, the report card aligns precisely with the literacy attributes, making it easy to construct. However, the biggest challenge lies in persuading teachers and administrators to break old habits (for example, mixing effort with performance, reporting on progress in what is taught instead of progress toward the attributes). And how to reform middle and high school report cards so they provide both traditional grades as well as evidence of progress toward the attributes remains problematic.

However, there's one more aspect of keeping track of and sharing students' literacy progress, and that is analyzing data from the various assessments to inform and improve the language arts curriculum. I now turn to that in the next chapter.

8

ANALYZING DATA TO INFORM INSTRUCTION

Thus far, we have discussed *literacy attributes* (what we want students to know and be able to do as readers, writers, speakers, listeners, viewers, and representers), *instructional contributions* (what we as teachers need to provide for students so they can acquire the attributes), *assessment* (keeping track of students' progress toward the attributes), and *reporting* (communicating with students, parents, colleagues, and the district about students' progress). This final part of the circle is all about *analyzing literacy data*.

If school districts do a terrible job of gathering literacy data, perhaps we shouldn't be surprised that they rarely analyze data or use data to inform instruction. It isn't that data aren't gathered. In fact, schools are required to amass huge amounts of data, especially under No Child Left Behind but also mandated by individual states; rather, it's that the data gathered can't easily be analyzed to inform teaching (as opposed to test preparation). Most of the data gathered by school districts are summative, norm-referenced achievement results. These include standardized reading achievement tests (for example, Terra Nova, Stanford Achievement Test, Metropolitan Achievement Test), mandated State Language Arts Assessments (for example, New York State's third- through eighth-grade ELA examinations, Massachusetts MCAS Reading Tests), and more detailed measures of aspects of literacy (for example, PALS, DIBELS [Dynamic Indicators of Basic Early Literacy Skills]).

Since No Child Left Behind legislation was passed, data from these measures have been gathered and scrutinized; the more detailed assessments (for example, DIBELS) have been analyzed (actually overanalyzed) to inform instruction, sometimes on a monthly or even weekly basis.

The problem here is that no matter how much one analyzes the reading achievement data, there is little that can be used to inform instruction, unless of course, one starts to align the literacy curriculum directly to the test content and format. Although the testmakers routinely warn against this, if the tests themselves become high-stakes measures, the temptation to teach to the test becomes overwhelming; indeed, that's exactly what happens. NCLB has made assessment a central focus of its mission, so school districts, even states, have made it theirs, too, with the result that reading achievement test data are being increasingly analyzed and used to drive instruction—drive, not inform.

I see this in action in the schools. In one school, the CBM (curriculum-based management, a measure of rapid decoding) is administered on a biweekly basis to students in remedial classes, and the results are used to continue or modify literacy instruction. This might be an exemplary practice if rapid decoding either was all that students needed to do or if (which is what's claimed) it inevitably leads to making sense of what is read. But it doesn't, according to the teachers at the next grade level; apparently, they are not the only ones who take issue with the claim that decoding speed inexorably leads to reading comprehension. A growing chorus of researchers argue that rapid decoding doesn't lead to understanding text, and it might not even lead to reading fluency.

So, if the data that are analyzed are either too broad (as in reading achievement tests) or too narrow (as in the CBM or DIBELS), and those data are rigorously gathered, analyzed, and put to use in instruction, the results might be misleading at best, quite dangerous at worst.

From a literacy attributes perspective, there are many shortcomings in both kinds of measures. For example, take a look at a typical reading achievement test and ask how well it covers the reading attributes. But typically these measures are used to assess students' achievement in literacy, not just reading, so it doesn't take much to realize that while they are "broad" in one sense (they provide overall comparisons between students in fairly vague categories), they are actually quite narrow in another sense (they rarely cover writing, let alone listening and speaking; they almost never measure viewing or representing).

Some state-mandated ELA assessments do a better job of covering important literacy areas. New York State, for example, samples reading and writing and, to some extent, listening. They certainly address literary understanding and not just reading comprehension. But they don't measure speaking.

Another issue with these measures, even the state-mandated ones, is that the results take so long to be returned to the school districts that even if the data could be used to inform instruction, it may be too late. I rarely see teachers even look at standardized reading achievement test scores, and until NCLB came along, most of the teachers I've worked with didn't spend much time looking at state ELA exam results, just a cursory glance to see who passed and who didn't and to breathe a sigh of relief that their scores were OK. That's changed recently. In one middle school, I noticed that Terra Novas (a literacy measure that mimics the New York ELA examination in content and format) were being administered every two weeks or so and the results "shared" (a euphemistic term, given that many of the young teachers receiving them were in tears) with teachers, with admonitions to get the scores up before the official tests were given. I see the same thing going on in elementary schools with the more detailed tests like DIBELS—regular testing, followed by "encouragements" to ensure that the test results improve.

When I think about analyzing literacy data to inform instruction, I'm thinking less about mining information from assessments to improve test performance and more about gathering data that can inform teachers' instructional contributions toward the attributes.

Gathering Data in an Attributes Approach

An attributes framework takes an entirely different approach to gathering and analyzing data. First of all, the data to be gathered do not simply consist of what's already mandated by NCLB or necessarily what's in use by the state or by teachers or specialists. Mandated literacy assessments play an important role in the attributes framework, one that will become clear presently, but they are not the primary data source.

So what data should be analyzed? The same data that are gathered to provide evidence for the report cards should be analyzed, but these are more likely to be raw data than those that appear on the report card. Data may also be gathered but not appear on the report card.

In the examples that follow, I want to describe the kinds of data that should be gathered across the literacy attributes and how these data might be mined by administrators and teachers to support students' growth toward them. I have chosen just a few attributes as examples. However, digging beneath the surface of what students reveal through their language (reading, writing, and so on) makes significant contributions to our understanding not only of their learning but also of our teaching.

Reads Widely

If teachers gathered evidence for the report cards largely through reading logs and then used these logs, along with a rubric, to assign a 1, 2, 3, or 4 on the report card under the heading Reads Widely, you would have two data sources. One would be the raw data, consisting of the logs themselves. The other would be the "derived" scores (1–4) on the report card.

The 1–4 scores, even though they are one step removed from the raw data, are still useful to analyze because they give a good indication of the amount and breadth of students' overall independent reading. If you are a teacher or principal in an elementary school, ask yourself this question: Could you lay your hands on data within the next few minutes that give even a rough picture of the extent of students' independent reading? I don't mean just one classroom; I mean *all* students in the school. And could you compare that, say, with other elementary schools in your district? Could you compare it with last year? Could you look at the amount and breadth of independent reading across time with a cohort of students?

If you can, then you already have implemented the kind of data gathering and analysis I am proposing here, even if you don't call it an attributes framework. But even so, the 1–4 scores aren't going to be sufficient, unless they are broken down into separate categories, which is highly unlikely on the report card. (Remember the principle of economy I discussed earlier in the book? We can't report on every aspect of literacy.)

Although the 1–4 scores (or whatever scoring system you use) are useful, the raw data can be even more useful. For example, when we talk about students reading widely, we typically mean reading across genres (fiction, nonfiction, poetry). So if one of our goals was, say, to increase the amount of nonfiction or poetry in the diet of students' independent reading, it might be interesting to examine reading logs to see the number and kind of readings separated into these genres. Again, the exercise will yield data that have important implications for instructional contributions. If you examine the reading log of the student presented in Exhibit 8.1, what does it say about the diet of this child's reading? What might examining the logs of a random sample of students within an entire grade reveal?

Suppose this analysis shows that despite professional development on broadening the genres read independently by students, there's still a huge bias in the reading logs toward fiction. Just sharing these data (without any identifiers that might cause embarrassment) will bring about a change in emphasis. It will also prompt thoughtful conversations about how best to balance genres and how accurately the reading logs record what students are reading. If the data are shared across grade levels, especially if sample reading

Exhibit 8.1. Example of Reading Log.

Benjamin 's Reading List Grade 3

Date Started / Date Ended	Title and Author	Type of Text — Fiction	Non-fiction	Poetry	Play	Other	How Read? — Alone	With partner or group	With Adult/Parent	Difficulty — Easy	Just right	Hard	Opinion — Didn't like 1	Okay 2	Good 3	Great 4	Your Comments
3/19 – 4/4	Hard Times on the Prairie Laura Wilder	X						X			X		1	2	3	(4)	This book was a great.
4/18 – 5/5	How to Be Cool in the third grade Betsy Duffy	X						X			X		1	2	(3)	4	This book was good!
5/14 – 9/9	Earthquake in the Early Morning Mary Pope Osborne	X					X	X			X		1	2	3	(4)	I like to read more nice books.
5/1 – 6/11	Batman National Geographic Explorer		X			Magazine	X	X			X		1	2	3	(4)	I would like to read more of the National.
6/12 – 6/15	Twister on Tuesday	X						X		X			1	2	3	(4)	I really loved it.

logs are distributed (again, without identifiers), more productive conversations will emerge, because teachers will start talking about issues across, rather than just within, grade levels. Often they find out that students are reading the same books in different grade levels—nothing wrong with that, if it's intentional!

From an administrator's perspective, these same data can be used in other ways. They can be aggregated to demonstrate student progress toward the literacy attributes or disaggregated to track progress—or lack of it—by groups of students (by gender, reading ability, ethnicity, grade), or even individual students. Suppose an analysis of the data shows that struggling readers are not only reading less than their peers; their reading is heavily biased toward lighter fictional works. This could be interpreted as problematic because the cumulative effect of less independent reading over several months or even years is known to be detrimental to their growth. And it might also be troubling that so much of their reading is fiction. But the fact that they are reading lighter works may be a sign that they are, in fact, reading material that's at their independent reading level, and we might be able to show that it's helping their reading fluency. At the same time, we may be limiting these struggling readers' exposure to and engagement in nonfiction, especially books with big ideas. How one interprets the data depends a lot on what the data are telling you, and they always need to be examined in context.

Decodes/Reads Fluently

A plethora of data can be—and more recently, are being— gathered on aspects of decoding fluency. One set of data relates to students' knowledge and facility with the various components of decoding, such as letter names, sound-symbol correspondence, phonemic awareness, phonics, sight words, and conventions or concepts of print. There are two primary ways of tapping this knowledge—one that asks students to recognize or name the components, the other that measures the rapidity or automaticity of the knowledge—in other words, *how rapidly* students can name letters, not merely *whether* they can name them.

The second set of data is all about the students' ability to fluently read connected text. This can be done by simply having students read aloud from books or other written material drawn from the classroom or by administering formal fluency measures, such as the DRA, which is untimed, or the CBM, which is timed.

Although many districts routinely gather many of these data, important questions can—and should—be asked. For example, what levels of performance are necessary on the individual component parts (for example, phonemic awareness, sight words, letter and letter-sound knowledge) in order to perform well on the measures of reading connected text? In Gilbertsville-Mt. Upton, we analyzed data from kindergarten and first grade that showed students with less-than-satisfactory scores on individual components scored perfectly well on the DRA. If reading fluency is the goal, and if the DRA measures that, then one instructional implication of these results is that perhaps we shouldn't be looking for mastery on individual components. Another might be that we should be spending more instructional time having students read connected text and less on the individual components. The small data set would obviously make us cautious about overgeneralizing, but it certainly raises questions we hadn't thought about before, and it suggests that gathering more data would be useful. Also, remember that when you analyze data from your own students (as opposed to simply implementing approaches based on other people's data), the implications relate to your situation in very meaningful ways.

A second analysis is to see what the relationship is between decoding fluency and comprehension, especially if the district has bought into the philosophy that one is a prerequisite to the other. If there are substantial numbers of students whose decoding fluency is strong but their comprehension is poor, and even a few whose comprehension is good but their decoding fluency is weak, then questions need to be raised about the correlation. I raise this because increasingly I see these anomalies in districts. I also understand that this same lack of correlation exists in preliminary studies of Reading First programs. Perhaps that shouldn't come as a surprise, when the correlations between decoding fluency and comprehension in studies quoted in the National Reading Panel (NICHD 2000) are not at all strong, either.

For me, the question is less about what research generally finds to be true than what is happening with students in particular schools. Most likely, an analysis of data in your school will yield mixed results. Some students will only perform well on decoding connected text when they've mastered most or all of the individual components. Others will read connected text fluently without having mastered the components. Trying to understand why and making adjustments to instructional contributions will make these analyses worthwhile. They will also inform teachers and specialists about techniques that seem to work well with students whose decoding profiles are similar.

This isn't to suggest that research findings are to be discounted in favor of local analysis of data, but that local analysis takes into account the specific characteristics of the students, teachers, and instructional practices. Data analysis should always include the latter, but be informed by the former.

Understands What Is Read

This attribute includes understanding informational and literary text, understanding big ideas, possessing an extensive reading vocabulary, and, in some projects, applying effective reading comprehension strategies.

Here the challenge is that few existing measures capture students' understanding of different kinds of texts, especially big ideas, although in New York State, the ELA examinations in third through eighth grade and the eleventh grade do a pretty good job of tapping these. There is much available data on students' vocabulary knowledge and comprehension strategies, particularly in traditional standardized achievement tests, but the comprehension strategies assessments reveal little about the strategies that students employ; rather they tap into whether students can answer literal or inferential questions on specially constructed passages.

Although the assessments and report cards in an attributes framework adequately measure the depth and breadth of students' understanding of texts, additional analyses of student work will reveal valuable information about how well students make sense of what they read and how instruction might be improved. For example, having students "think aloud" the strategies they use to make sense of a complex poem or short story may reveal that they don't simply apply the strategies taught to them by teachers or that they misunderstand what they've been taught. However, there's always the question about whether the reason students don't understand is because they haven't read enough or that they haven't understood or sufficiently applied the taught strategies. Here is where gathering data from student assignments, discussions with students, and conversations with colleagues can illuminate this issue.

Writing

Some aspects of writing cry out for careful analysis. It is well known that students perform better on spelling and grammar tests than they employ correct spelling and grammar in their compositions. In fact, parents frequently complain that their children receive high scores for these on report cards, yet their writing is full of errors. It would be useful to be able to analyze written compositions to see what the relation is between understanding spelling and grammar rules and actually using them (this may be a function of imperfect rules, imperfect instruction, or imperfect learning) and, again, whether spelling and grammar improve or become acceptable primarily through other means—for example, writing a great deal, writing workshops, or various kinds of feedback. If there were insights to be gained through these analyses, instructional practices would be vastly improved.

Other aspects of writing, for example language and style, are much more difficult constructs, and careful analyses of how professional writers use language to create effects on readers and how students learn these same techniques might be very useful. The work of Katie Wood Ray is particularly relevant here, as she has engaged students in such studies. How effectively other teachers might use similar techniques and what happens when students employ them is an open question. Yet if we are to help students acquire this attribute, we need to learn a great deal more about the instructional strategies and how effective they are with students of varying writing abilities and varying writing experiences.

Communicates Ideas Effectively Through Speaking

Speaking involves communicating meaning, but it also involves technique (volume, pitch, gestures). Some districts I work with also include "reading expressively" in this attribute. The assessment of this attribute typically involves a rubric to use when listening to students speak in various settings and for various purposes. Some of the data I wish we had gathered before doing the rubric (and spending hours arguing about how to weigh the various techniques) include an analysis of video samples of students speaking, to tease out which techniques seem to influence listeners most in determining the effectiveness of speaking and whether different techniques weigh more heavily, say, in reading aloud, as opposed to making a presentation. Knowing about these not only will help make better judgments in assessments; more important, they will inform how best to coach students as they improve their speaking abilities.

Summary

In the projects I have done with schools, we rarely get to the stage where data is systematically analyzed and used to inform instruction, let alone inform the entire attributes framework. This is mostly due to the overwhelming pressure on school districts to perform well on national or state assessments, so that the bulk of data analyses is devoted to these. I hope that the case I have made in this chapter might persuade school administrators to pay more attention to analyzing literacy attributes data, because what is learned can be applied directly to improving instruction, which in turn leads to better outcomes. The challenge lies in how to gather the data in an efficient manner so that it doesn't become a burden on teachers, and to analyze it quickly enough it so it can be used in a timely fashion. None of the schools I have worked with have yet accomplished this, but I remain optimistic that it can be done, and convinced that it should be.

This chapter closes the circle that encompasses literacy attributes, instructional contributions, instructional support, assessment and reporting, and, finally, analyzing data.

In the next chapter, I want to describe the process of making this happen in schools.

9

IMPLEMENTING THE FRAMEWORK

In this chapter, I want to share some ideas about implementing an attributes framework, culled from many years' experience in a variety of public schools in the Northeast. Over time, I have come to realize that if a new way of thinking about language arts is to prevail, especially in America's public schools, it has to build on what is already in place, and it has to encompass the full range of components that make up a language arts program in a district, from articulating the language arts goals, to instruction, to assessment and reporting. Just tinkering with one of these is not enough. The politics of a district and community must be navigated. Many would-be reformers complain that if only a district had more faithfully implemented *their* approach, the reforms would have been more successful. A better interpretation may be that the reforms themselves demanded more than a district was willing or able to carry out or that the reforms weren't fully thought out.

The Process of Articulating Literacy Attributes

First, I want to share some techniques for articulating literacy attributes. These have evolved over the years from a laborious, painful, time-consuming process (it took over two years in the late 1980s to arrive at reading attributes for exiting eighth-graders in Manchester Elementary School in Manchester Center, Vermont) to a thoughtful but relatively quick exercise to articulate K–12 literacy attributes, as well as appropriate instructional contributions and assessments in Gilbertsville-Mt. Upton, New York, in 2003–2005. Practice doesn't make perfect, but it certainly improves the quality of the results and time-to-completion.

Let me describe the process I use to help a school district articulate its literacy attributes. In doing so, I'll collapse several projects into one, so that I can better illustrate both what seems to work well and what obstacles I've encountered. However, this process cannot get under way without some careful preparation, such as understanding what is already in place, establishing a scope and sequence for implementing the framework, creating a language arts committee, and agreeing on the framework itself. Because these are critical steps, let me start with them.

Getting to Know What's Already in Place

Many school districts embark on new initiatives without first taking stock of where they are in language arts. In most schools I work with, I'm reluctant to help with a reform before I've had an extensive opportunity to understand what's already in place and to share that understanding with the district. In fact, the reason for my being in a district in the first place is typically because there's dissatisfaction with what's going on in language arts—either test scores are disappointing, or new initiatives aren't working as well as planned, or the district simply wants a fresh pair of eyes looking at its entire language arts programs, pre-K through grade 12 (or some smaller part of it).

Whether this first stage is called an audit or a study (*study* is a less threatening term than *audit*), its purpose is to learn as much as possible about the district's language arts philosophy, its curriculum, classroom practices, and assessment. This can be accomplished in one of two ways, sometimes both together. One is to ask an outside consultant to spend time in the district, talking with teachers, specialists, administrators, students, and parents about the language arts programs, observing language arts instruction, reviewing curriculum documents, and examining assessments and literacy test data. Another is to engage the district in a self-study, preferably led by the same group that will be implementing the framework. Combining the two is also quite productive: engaging the district in a thoughtful self-study, then following that up with an external review.

The process of articulating literacy expectations must start with a good understanding of the current language arts philosophy, existing expectations, the major instructional and assessment practices, and what district members report as strengths and concerns. Not only does this provide clear indications of what needs working on, it also ensures that whatever comes next is built on what is already there. How we frame literacy expectations, instructional contributions, assessment, and reporting depends a great deal on knowing how each component is currently defined and implemented. Also, there's always a greater buy-in to any project that respects what is in place. Of course, in some districts, what is already there is so dysfunctional that there's little to build on. At least a study will reveal this, so one can plan accordingly.

Determining the Scope of the Project

Before it can articulate literacy expectations, the district has to decide the scope of the project. Should it focus on K–12? Include pre-K or even preschool? Start with elementary and get that done first before moving on to the upper grades? Focus only on language arts or also include literacy across the curriculum? Involve library media specialists? Include special education? The broader the scope, the more likely a district will eventually generate a seamless set of literacy expectations, instructional contributions, and assessments from at least K–12, ideally earlier than kindergarten. But stretching this far brings with it the danger of overstretching and inadequately attending to the design and implementation of the components. A more serious danger is that the district will move on to other initiatives, either because of traditionally short attention spans for school reforms or because of changes in upper administration. Sadly, new administrators rarely want to carry on where their predecessors left off. I try to help a district make realistic expectations for the scope and duration of a project, but there are always unexpected circumstances that disrupt the most carefully laid plans.

A district may opt to start completely from scratch or begin by reviewing attributes, instructional contributions, and assessments from previous projects. Recently, I've noticed that districts increasingly choose to start with literacy attributes that other districts have already created. I have mixed feelings about this. On the one hand, it is much easier to adopt and adapt what others have done. It also takes a great deal less time, which is a critical variable. But it also has a constraining effect. Once the overall frame has been established, modifying it becomes much more difficult. In fact, in earlier projects, if we hadn't started from scratch, I'm not sure we would have solved a number of serious issues that stemmed from partially or poorly conceived elements of the framework. Maybe what has happened is that over the course of several projects, a robust framework has emerged that doesn't need overhauling, just adapting to local situations. But I still worry about this.

A second option pertains to the order in which the framework elements are to be worked on. Obviously, articulating literacy attributes has to come first. But after that, it's a toss-up whether to move to instructional contributions or assessment. I've done it both ways. Tackling assessment before instructional contributions has two benefits. One stems from the oft-repeated but true dictum that assessment drives instruction, so if you have assessments in place, instructional contributions aligned with those assessments will come quickly. There's nothing like having to report on a student's progress in a specific area to ensure that the area is covered in the classroom. Also, it's awkward working on new instructional contributions while at the same time having teachers complete outdated report cards.

However, in recent projects, districts have opted to work on instructional contributions before revising the assessments. I can see their point. They think that teachers need to be comfortable with their teaching routines before asking them to track students' progress toward the attributes, especially in areas they might not already be confident, such as understanding big ideas, viewing, or representing. An added benefit is having sufficient examples of student work so there is adequate evidence sitting behind the new assessments. In one district, we got around the problem of new instructional contributions versus old report cards by piloting new assessments alongside the existing ones. This worked very well, and I suspect that in all future projects the instructional contributions phase will come ahead of the assessments.

Sometimes, decisions on the scope and sequence are made by district administrators prior to the start of a project; sometimes they are left to the project members to decide. In any event, the next important task is to create a small working group to initiate the language arts project.

Creating a Language Arts Committee. The key here is to create a language arts committee that represents significant stakeholders. The size and composition of the group needs careful thought. There shouldn't be more than ten to fifteen members. Fewer than that, representation suffers; greater than that, meaningful progress is hard to achieve. In addition to ensuring representation of grades and roles (teachers, specialists, administrators, parents), I like to ensure that different points of view are also represented. All too often, language arts committees are populated by like-minded educators, but if opposing viewpoints are not represented during the early stages of a project, they'll eventually have to be confronted anyway; by then, opponents will be much harder to bring around. But there are more cogent reasons to include them. Call them naysayers or old-fashioned, whole-language or direct instruction—or whatever—their views derive from and parallel those found in the research and professional literature. Including them in the group ensures that different points of view are both represented and engaged. The long-term success of any project rests, in part, on the productive conversations among legitimately different perspectives.

But I also try to seek out participants who have leadership roles (self- or other-assigned) in their schools, regardless of the views they hold on language arts. Because the ultimate goal of these projects is to effect meaningful change, including these participants is a smart proposition.

If we try to represent all grade levels, all kinds of roles, all viewpoints, and all power brokers, the size of the committee will definitely exceed the recommended upper limit. The way to prevent this is to hold to the ten to fifteen members and have participants either wear two hats or represent more than one grade level.

Sometimes, it makes sense to use an existing language arts committee. If it already adequately represents grades, roles, and points of view, that's fine. If not, it can be modified. If it's a committee that can't easily be modified, then it's better to start from scratch. I've had projects fail because the district insisted we use an existing committee, made up largely of administrators. The projects that have yielded the best results have always started with a group that fully represents grades, roles, and points of view.

Laying Out the Framework. I start a new project by meeting with the language arts committee, preferably in the presence of the senior administrators, to either lay out the scope and sequence of the project or, if left to the committee, to decide these. I begin by laying out the framework (see Exhibit 1.1) and the communication triangle (see Exhibit 1.2) that provides its underpinnings. Because the framework itself has to become non-negotiable, taking the time to describe each of the components, especially how they relate to each other, is a critical step. I don't want to get too far into the project if the framework that guides and defines it is unacceptable. Interestingly, the reaction to the framework, especially once all its components were in place, has been uniformly positive in all the schools I've worked with, including those that ultimately failed to follow through on the language arts reforms.

I ascribe this to its simplicity and the ease with which it relates to language arts as it's taught and assessed in their classrooms and school. Mostly, however, it's because the framework itself comes from working on these projects with educators over a number of years in a variety of school settings.

Articulating Literacy Attributes. Once we have completed all the preparatory work, know where the district is in language arts, have a representative language arts committee with about fifteen members, and the overall framework is agreeable to everyone, we can start articulating literacy attributes. For the sake of argument, suppose we have decided to start the process of articulating literacy attributes without the benefit of someone else's attributes in front of us. And suppose we have agreed to make them K–12 and, at least to begin with, will try to articulate expectations for all grade levels together rather than individually.

The first step, then, is to articulate the language arts components within which to create our expectations. I like to present them within the *receptive* and *expressive* categories, so that (1) "receptive" includes *reading* (making sense of what is read), *listening* (making sense of what is heard), and *viewing* (making sense of what is observed), and (2) "expressive" includes *writing* (expressing ideas in written form), *speaking* (expressing ideas in spoken form), and *representing* (expressing ideas in a variety of media). Immediately, questions will arise about the uniqueness of each of the components. Aren't writing and speaking simply two forms of representation? Isn't reading one form of viewing? The answers to both questions is, of course, yes. And in fact, I tried in one district to collapse speaking and writing into representation. The idea appealed to some for a short while, but it wasn't long before the three components were separated again. In truth, all three *are* just different forms of representation, but in the minds of most educators, they are quite separable.

Two other issues typically arise here. One is discomfort about the addition of viewing and representing as components of language arts. This is especially the case in New York State, whose English/ Language Arts Standards do not include viewing or representing. Yet, increasingly, New York's literacy and content-area assessments require students to view and represent, so in recent years, including them as components has required less arm-twisting. Including these in preschool and pre-K projects is a no-brainer.

The other issue that sometimes comes up is whether we can legitimately differentiate between the components, given how interrelated they are. In fact, New York State's English/Language Arts Standards articulate these components in a much more related fashion by organizing them underneath a purpose (they could easily have included *view* and *represent* here):

- Standard 3: Students will read, write, listen, and speak for critical analysis and evaluation.

In a couple of districts, we actually tried to organize the components in a more related way, but in the end, keeping them as separate components for the purpose of articulating expectations prevailed, especially when it was pointed out that the instructional contributions do not need to be—in fact, should not be—carried out as separate components. (I discussed this issue in Chapter Three in the section on containers for language arts instruction).

The next step is to propose attributes within each of the components. In an effort to ward off huge lists of skills, I set out some guidelines. An attribute, I tell committee members, is what skill, knowledge, ability, or experience that we think a student should possess as a reader, writer, speaker, listener, viewer, or representer. So, it isn't just about skills.

One critical feature of attributes is that they represent the most important or critical expectations, not all of them. We can always tuck less important or contributing skills underneath the critical ones, and we can also distinguish between attributes and contributions to attributes. An *attribute* is an important manifestation of an accomplished language user. A *contribution* is what we teach or engage students in to ensure good progress toward an attribute.

Another way of defining an attribute is to think of it as an outer-layer manifestation; lesser or contributing skills can be described as inner-layer. It's not an easy concept, because any skill could be defined both ways. For example, the attribute "decodes fluently" could be an outer-layer manifestation of early reading but an inner-layer contributor to "understands what is read." Deciding the boundaries of outer and inner layers has to be negotiated with the participants, but over time, I've noticed increasing agreement on where those boundaries should be.

The other thing I remind committee members about as we start this process is that articulating things simply is enormously difficult and typically quite frustrating. It isn't just the difficulty in deciding what's really important; it's abandoning the usual practice of assembling and listing every possible language arts skill.

So, with these reminders in hand, we typically start on reading attributes, working with the entire group, listing what everyone thinks are the most critical attributes, and then going back to the lists to see if they represent our expectations (this is where having kindergarten teachers working alongside secondary English teachers produces lively and productive conversations); we try to see how best to shorten the lists to avoid any redundancy and to ensure that only what's most important survives the revision process. I normally take one component and work it right through with the group so that they see the process in action, see what happens as a large list is transformed into a small one, but, most important, understand that this is less about making lists than it is about productive professional conversation about what we want our students to accomplish in literacy. As I reflect on these workshops, the thing that stands out are the comments made by participants about how the discussions really made them think about what's important to them, something that rarely happens in curriculum committee meetings.

In between meetings of the language arts committee, members return to their buildings, share what they have been constructing, and bring back reactions and suggestions from colleagues. This helps our work in two ways: (1) it communicates the framework and the developing attributes to colleagues, and (2) it returns to the committee helpful suggestions about specific attributes or issues. However, just because a suggestion is made doesn't mean that it will automatically result in an addition or change. All contributions from within and outside the committee are subjected to discussion and revisions. If they weren't, we'd end up with more and more attributes. Saying no—respectfully—is an important principle in creating attributes. However, ignoring suggestions is not an option, either. And just in case you think that, as the consultant, I have the last word, I do not. I will argue the case for simplicity, for tucking things in, for not being redundant, for not ignoring literacy experiences (for example, reads widely), but in the final analysis, the attributes belong to the district, and I will be long gone by the time a student graduates within the framework they have implemented. Also, I have to say that the very best suggestions for attributes and their wording have come from colleagues, not from me. It's not easy for consultants to be good listeners, but professional growth emerges from productive conversations, not monologues.

Once the language arts committee has agreed on a draft of all the attributes, they are compiled into a document and then shared with the entire school community for reaction and comment. In the early projects, this was done by hand and laboriously summarized. Recently, I have discovered Web-based surveys through *surveymonkey.com* that are incredibly easy to construct, accessible through any Web browser, and tallied in real time. Literally, within minutes of respondents completing their surveys, I can deliver to the language arts committee a detailed analysis of both numerical and comment data (see Exhibit 9.1).

We use these surveys for two purposes. One is to solicit feedback on the attributes. We take this feedback very seriously, and there's always something significant that gets changed as a consequence of a suggestion, often made by a single respondent. We also get to see which components and attributes sit most comfortably

Exhibit 9.1. Example from SurveyMonkey.

Specific comments, concerns, or questions about LISTENING attributes and/or non-negotiables:

1. This is probably the most important skill that can be taught in the early grades.

2. Considering other points of view is an idea that intersects with development of cross-cultural communication skills

3. While I agree that the listening generally makes sense, again I do not feel that I have adequate time in a day to fully allow for the kind of listening "lessons" that need to be taught on a daily basis. We keep adding more to our curriculum and are forgetting about the basics. I believe our tests scores reflect this harried schedule and overdone curriculum we are all living. As an aside, the district also needs to address the numbers of children who are coming to us that need specialized services at an early level. If we truly believe in early intervention then we need to provide early intervention.

4. Must take into account the child's developmental stage, especially the young child who is not always able to take others' perspectives

5. These attributes are important. Unfortunately, the district has bogged the classroom down with an extensive "push down" curriculum, which impedes any substantial/meaningful practice of these skills. Fragmented instructional days do not allow for a meaningful exchange or analysis of ideas.

6. There should be a large part of the curriculum devoted to listening.

7. How can we help ELL in this area in a more concrete way?

8. In regards to listening skills, it is important to take into consideration the educational environment in which the child is placed.

9. Listening is a skill that every child needs to develop to be successful in a challenging academic world.

10. Of course, listening assumes the child knows the sound system of the language; it is integral to literacy.

11. This is directly from the NYS standards a curriculum map is what is needed. We already know the standards.

12. Students need to practice LISTENING at home. Families should be encouraged to begin helping the child at an early age. Listening is critical for learning anything.

13. In order to enhance one's ability to listen and to understand what is heard, multiple types (i.e., different senses) of information need to be delivered simultaneously. Oftentimes, "listening" doesn't occur in isolation.

14. Needs exemplars

15. I find this to be an area of weakness in many children. I find myself spending a lot of time on checking for understanding after directions have been given.

16. "Listening with empathy" is not the most user-friendly phrase. Focus on respectfully interpreting a variety of viewpoints.

17. Very important life skill!

18. I myself have related listening to paying attention and following directions. What I have found was that even if the students are listening, they still do not comprehend what is being asked of them just because they hear the words that I or a peer is saying. Being able to analyze and understand what they are hearing is a skill that I myself have to work on with my students. By providing a variety of voices and purposes I feel this goal can be obtained.

19. Crucial element.

among colleagues at different grade levels. This information is very useful in terms of areas that need more explanation or in some cases more attention in classrooms. Viewing and representing are frequently regarded in our surveys as questionable areas for attributes. Yet later in the implementation, educators become very attached to them. So there's not a direct relationship between what shows up on surveys and what gets revised, added, or dropped.

The second purpose is a little less obvious but equally important. You can see that an attribute, once agreed on, drives the entire framework: it is a goal of the language arts program; it requires specific instructional contributions; it's going to be tracked, and it's going to show up on the report card. If we have trivial attributes, then we'll be making a huge commitment to supporting students' growth in them and spend time assessing them and reporting them to parents. Of course, many districts have goals that are never seriously tied to instructional contributions and don't show up on the report card, so it really doesn't matter what the goals are, because the focus will be on skills that *do* appear on the report card.

In this framework, however, everything is linked, so getting the attributes right is a very serious matter. As we are working on the attributes, we stress this, but there will always be teachers who, remembering prior language arts reforms that didn't go anywhere, glibly fill in the surveys without reflecting on what they mean, having little faith that they will actually go anywhere. Later, when we get to the assessments, these teachers may come out of the woodwork to complain that they were never consulted. I know this has happened on several occasions. It's nice to be able to respond that they were consulted and that their suggestions were taken seriously. But suggestions never made cannot be acted upon.

I say this not to be critical. I don't blame teachers for being cynical about reforms that come and go. Rather, I say it to emphasize a process that takes sharing and feedback seriously. At some point, everyone starts to realize that the framework is going to be implemented, and they become more involved and more committed to the process. It's what I call the inevitability factor. Up until this happens, many people don't fully engage because they see no point in it. But when they see that it's worthwhile, they do. And that's when good things really start to happen. And by "good things," I don't mean slavishly following what I or others have suggested. I mean enjoining the conversation with a view toward setting the right goals and creating the best instructional contributions to accomplish them. And keeping it simple.

Publishing a Working Set of Attributes. The final step in the process is to review the suggestions made by colleagues across the district and publish a working set of attributes. It's a working set, because there are two more components—instructional contributions and assessments—to come, and as these are developed, further modifications to the attributes may have to be made. However, having a clear notion of the literacy expectations for the chosen levels (for example, pre-K through grade 12) allows these next two stages to get under way.

The other thing I typically recommend at this stage is to present the working set of literacy attributes to the central administration and ask them to share them with the Board of Education. This serves several purposes: it legitimizes the entire framework; it lets the board know that the project has already yielded a set of clear, simple expectations, and it allows us to use the board approval as a counter to those who might be thinking that the project is simply the consultant's vision of language arts rather than the district's. In fact, this came into play recently in a district, where some deeply divided opinions about how to proceed with both instructional contributions and assessment were beginning to unravel the entire project. We were able to share with the language arts committee that the overall philosophy and direction of the project had already been decided by the Board of Education and that the committee's responsibility was to proceed within that direction and philosophy, not to subvert it. Being able to refer to decisions made by the Board of Education was particularly helpful in resolving what could have undermined the entire effort. (However, it does raise some questions that I'll come back to in Chapter Ten).

Articulating Instructional Contributions. The process of articulating instructional contributions starts with creating the non-negotiables. (*Non-negotiable contributions* represent instruction and experiences that every teacher and specialist must provide all students, as I discussed in Chapter Three). The first is to brainstorm them for each of the attributes (for example, "reads widely") or subattributes (for example, "decodes fluently"). I am always surprised when we do this how many of these initial suggestions either don't relate to the attribute or do advocate a particular instructional strategy that a teacher uses and thinks that everyone else should, too. However, once we get into the exercise, the number of irrelevant suggestions decreases, and the few, critical ones start to emerge and coalesce.

At this stage, I don't worry too much about the specific wording or the fact that suggestions overlap. Sometimes, we do this exercise as a whole group, using a smartboard or large chart paper. Sometimes, it seems to work better with educators working in small groups, then sharing their non-negotiables with the whole group.

The next step, preferably done a few days after the brainstorming to allow for reflection, is to examine the suggested non-negotiables and start revising them so that they cover the critical contributions, without any overlap between them. At this stage, we also work on the wording, to make sure that it says what we want, in as simple and clear language as we can. This step is very hard, but it's necessary and always results in deeper thinking about what's important.

Finally, the draft set of non-negotiables is typed up and sent out to all faculty and administrators for their review and comment. As with the attributes, the feedback is carefully considered, and a final set of attributes, with their accompanying non-negotiable instructional contributions, is published. As with the literacy attributes, I like to pass these on to the central administration and to the Board of Education for their review and approval.

The second task is drafting the instructional activities. (*Instructional activities* represent the accommodations needed to address the particular strengths and needs of diverse students, as well as put to good use the craft and expertise of individual teachers. Instructional activities also represent legitimately different instructional methods and materials to achieve common goals; see Chapter Three). There are two primary ways to accomplish this. One is for the language arts committee to provide examples of instructional activities and place them underneath the listings of non-negotiables. What this does is give real-world examples of the kinds of activities that teachers can use to implement the non-negotiables, without specifying too many of them and thereby overloading the document with details. Further, it makes much clearer what "counts" as an activity that supports the non-negotiables. This is important, because I've found that many teachers like to fit the activities they already do into the non-negotiables, whether they are relevant or not. Providing examples is a good way of promoting relevance.

The other way to articulate instructional activities is to have teachers at grade levels construct their own "maps" or charts to relate non-negotiables to instructional activities. What I like about this strategy is that it grounds the non-negotiables in the day-to-day activities and experiences that teachers engage their students in and helps make the entire exercise useful in terms of daily planning. Often these curriculum exercises look good on paper but don't transfer into daily teaching; yet if the framework doesn't actually influence what happens in classrooms, what's the point of it?

Also, the whole idea here is that there are common expectations (attributes), common instructional contributions (non-negotiables), but flexible and appropriate instructional activities. By having teachers work on relating their instructional activities to the non-negotiables and to the attributes, specific to their own language arts program, we can expect much better implementation of the entire framework. Yet providing a small number of examples of instructional activities within the language arts documents helps everyone understand the relationship between non-negotiables and instructional activities, without making these documents too detailed and bulky.

Another strategy that has worked well for articulating instructional activities is to conduct workshops with teachers at grade levels. If you take each of the non-negotiables in turn and ask teachers to say what they currently do to implement them, you'll find that much of what we want to have happen is already taking place. However, you'll also discover that in many instances, teachers really don't understand what the non-negotiables are calling for, or they think that instructional activities they engage students in are related to non-negotiables, when in fact they really aren't. Workshops like these are very helpful in making clearer what the non-negotiables really mean and how to ensure that instructional activities relate to them. Yet they also privilege and confirm practices that teachers already employ in their classrooms, so what's new builds on what's already in place. I am not shy about praising teachers for the wonderfully relevant and thoughtful activities they use in their classrooms and am surprised to learn sometimes that no one else has noticed or commented on them. But I also use these opportunities to share examples (typically drawn from good practices I've observed in other classrooms) of activities that might better support the non-negotiable contributions. Simply articulating examples of activities in curriculum documents or creating binders full of lesson plans isn't enough. What's needed is to change the whole dynamic of how instructional contributions should be made that are flexible, on the one hand, but support the non-negotiables on the other.

I do have to insert a comment here about curriculum mapping. Curriculum mapping is a technique for articulating curriculum objectives, instructional activities, skills, student outcomes, and assessments (Jacobs 1997; Jacobs 2004). Curriculum mapping has become very popular in schools as a mechanism for creating, archiving, and reviewing curriculum across all subject areas. And with the advent of Web-based curriculum-mapping software, its popularity has increased dramatically in the past few years.

I have mixed feelings about curriculum mapping. On the one hand, mapping seems to work well in laying out instructional units that are tied to what are called "essential questions" (for example, What happens when belief systems of societies and individuals come into conflict? How can language be powerful? What can I learn about friends and friendships from the novels we read in school?).

The problem is that an essential question isn't the same as an attribute, so while other aspects of curriculum maps are compatible (for example, curriculum aligned with essential questions, assessment aligned with curriculum, everything aligned to state learning standards), these maps have a different starting point than attributes. I think curriculum mapping works much better at the secondary level, where "essential questions" do indeed drive instruction in content areas. Unfortunately, language arts is not a content area, so trying to create essential questions out of language processes becomes quite problematic and language arts curriculum maps frequently end up with skills (for example, main idea) or even genres (fiction, nonfiction, poetry) as essential questions. In an attributes framework, these skills are tucked inside broader categories (for example, understanding a main idea is tucked inside "understands informational or literary text"; genres are tucked inside attributes such as "reads widely.")

I have actually tried to reconcile attribute and curriculum mapping frameworks in a district that implemented both at the same time. I failed. In the end, that district ended up with curriculum mapping and abandoned the attributes framework. I am now thinking that curriculum mapping needs to be thought of as a powerful tool for articulating and recording *instructional activities* related to content, but it makes a poor substitute framework for literacy attributes. In other words, curriculum mapping should be a sub-component of an attributes framework, not the framework itself.

Making Non-Negotiables Non-Negotiable. I recall vividly in a neighboring school district that the superintendent, a loyal follower of Madeline Hunter, insisted that all teachers take the Hunter training and use Hunter's instructional techniques in the classroom. I knew one of the teachers (she was in our master's program), and she did not care for Madeline Hunter's notions of "good" teaching. She thought they were too behavioristic. So she set about making this non-negotiable negotiable by scheduling a doctor's appointment on the Hunter training-session day in her building. That didn't work; she found herself signed up for a make-up session in another building. Again she scheduled an appointment with her doctor. This time, it worked. Since that time, no one asked her to attend a training session, and neither was she observed or written up for not using, for example, Hunter's anticipatory sets. This wait-it-out strategy works just as well with an attributes approach.

Of course, one obvious way of ensuring that the non-negotiables are implemented in each and every classroom is to build them into the observation criteria for supervisors. Certainly, it makes no sense to have teachers observed using a scheme that has nothing to do with the attributes framework (for example, looking only at whether certain audiovisuals are used in teaching). But if the goal is to have the non-negotiables fully implemented, then they have to be part of the fabric of every classroom and an integral part of what teachers want to undertake for themselves. Although a coercive, or worse, punitive approach may produce lip-service compliance, it rarely lasts beyond the tenure of a supervisor and often, as in my earlier example, even less time than that.

I think there are several ways that non-negotiables can be implemented. One is to build them into the way teachers plan their instruction, both long range (a year) and short term (weekly or daily). The attributes and their non-negotiables are not aligned in the sense that they are not taught as isolated lessons; a plan book cannot simply be laid out with attributes and non-negotiables on one side and instructional activities on the other. Instead, teachers need to consult the attributes and non-negotiables as they prepare instructional activities, regardless of the containers they use for implementing them. So in a theme-based approach, a teacher would know that she has to balance fiction, nonfiction, and poetry in the selection of read-alouds, shared or guided reading, and independent reading. This could be done within a theme or across themes. In fact, it will probably work better across themes, because some themes lend themselves better to poetry and fiction, while others might want to emphasize nonfiction. The non-negotiables have to be implemented, not in every lesson or day or week but across the whole year.

If teachers develop a method for representing the attributes and non-negotiables in their planning books, then it shouldn't be difficult for a supervisor to examine these to ensure that non-negotiables are represented appropriately.

Then, in observing in the classroom, supervisors should be able to see how the instructional activities represent the non-negotiables in practice and how well teachers do things like differentiate instruction, engage students, work within their zone of proximal development, and so on. There needs to be a thread that links attributes to non-negotiables to instructional activities, even when the containers in which instruction takes place are completely different from one another.

Supervisors can also examine the extent to which teachers are moving students toward the attributes and how they are accomplishing this. It may be that there's a logical thread between the observed instructional activities and the non-negotiables, but a student is making little or no progress. Perhaps it's time for a more differentiated instructional strategy.

Another, perhaps more powerful, tool for ensuring that non-negotiables are implemented is by establishing a teaching environment in the school where teachers reflect, on their own and with colleagues, on the non-negotiables and how best to implement them. Sharing instructional strategies and activities, and especially student work (for example, samples of writing, videotapes of classroom interactions) yields insights; so does bringing to a group some case studies of students who seem not to be benefiting from the instructional activities currently being employed. It takes quite a while to build an environment in which this sharing can take place with everyone feeling comfortable, but once established, it builds ownership among the very educators who will be with the students over the longest period of time.

For me, the greatest challenge in an attributes project is to persuade administrators to stay focused on the attributes and non-negotiables long enough to see them fully implemented. If the focus is lost, all too quickly teachers lose that focus, too, and they'll never get to a point where they understand how to connect attributes to non-negotiables to instructional activities (and vice versa) and so won't own the process themselves.

Spreading the Responsibility. We tend to think of administrators as the primary enforcers of a district policy, but as I have hinted, teachers themselves are much better enforcers, once they understand and own the framework. However, other stakeholders can play a vital role in enforcement, too.

Once parents understand the system, especially if they like it and see their children benefit from it, they will actively monitor what is going on and reinforce the instructional activities. One way to help them is to provide them with a parent guide that explains in clear, lay terms the district's language arts philosophy, its attributes, non-negotiables, and examples of instructional activities. The guide also needs to walk parents through the assessments and report cards. Finally, it should suggest to parents practical ways in which they can contribute to their children's literacy attributes. A guide by itself won't ensure that all parents make appropriate contributions, but it's a start.

Surprisingly, students themselves are good monitors of how the framework is implemented. An example from first grade: a teacher had implemented a chart to list all the books she read aloud to the children. By each title, she listed (and discussed with the children) its genre—fiction, nonfiction, poetry. After doing this for a while, a child piped up during the morning meeting: "How come there are a lot of books in the 'fiction' column and almost none in the 'nonfiction'?" It didn't take the teacher long to get the hint. Within a week or so, the list started to be better balanced!

Spreading the responsibility also can involve teachers in other curriculum areas. I have already remarked that this is a difficult challenge, and I worry that it often becomes a matter of trying to persuade music and art teachers to become reading teachers. However, engaging teachers in other subject areas in conversations about what they can contribute to the language arts non-negotiables and what language arts instructional activities can contribute to subject-area learning, it always works better if the contributions are reciprocal, that is, can be mutually rewarding for both teachers and students.

Finally, don't forget that outside of school, there are many places and people who contribute to students' literacy development, ranging from public libraries, to businesses, to social service agencies, and especially programs that have direct responsibility for nurturing children's and parents' literacy (for example, Head Start, Even Start, Migrant Education, Literacy Volunteers). Getting to know people in these institutions and programs and engaging them in the same way one might engage with colleagues in the school district itself (How can we help each other?) will yield important insights about the contributions they already make to students and their parents outside the school. It will also help them broaden their definition of literacy and give them ideas about instructional activities that can support their work, as well as support the children's school literacy expectations.

We all glibly mouth, "It takes the whole village to raise the child," but until we engage and interact with the whole village, the maxim is hollow and meaningless. However, once we embrace all those who play a role in supporting literacy, wherever it is practiced, there is no limit to the progress that can be made.

Assessing and Reporting

The third major task in an attributes framework is deciding on how to gather evidence, analyze it, and report on student progress toward the literacy attributes.

This is a task for the language arts committee. I typically start by proposing the set of assessment principles I described in Chapter Six for the committee to discuss:

- We need to know where *all* students are, relative to *all* the literacy attributes.
- *All* literacy assessments should relate to, and provide information on, each student's progress toward the literacy attributes.
- Local school- or districtwide literacy assessments should be used primarily to inform and improve instruction but also should contribute to reporting grade-level, schoolwide, and districtwide progress in literacy to the school community.
- Mandated State English/Language Arts examinations are a critical aspect of a district's literacy assessment but should not be used as the sole or primary yardstick of progress toward literacy attributes.
- Assessments should be economical and, wherever possible, be embedded within regular classroom instruction.
- Assessments should draw on observations, conversations, and analysis of samples of literacy behaviors, not just literacy tasks or tests.
- Formal literacy assessments should have best available reliability and validity.

Once these principles are accepted (as-is or with revisions on the basis of the discussion), we then decide on how best to organize the assessment phase of the project. I like to think about what we want to end up with and then work backwards from there. We know we'll have to deliver new or revised report cards for the elementary grades and either new or revised interims for the secondary schools. And to go along with these, we'll need guides for teachers to use as they gather information and analyze it in order to complete the report cards or interims.

I like to focus on the deliverables, not only because that's what we have to work toward but also because they represent concrete progress toward completing the project. Even in draft form, assessment guides and mock-ups of report cards are as motivating to teachers and administrators as an architect's scale drawings and models are to a prospective house owner. (As each draft is completed, I like to lay it out the way it might look in its final format and use these as the basis for further revisions.)

Before we start creating the guides and report cards or interims, we have to decide on how many guides and reports there are going to be. Some divisions are obvious (the secondary interims have to be separate), but some are not so clear-cut: often, the pre-K and kindergarten classes use one format; grades 1 and 2 and grades 3 through 6 use different ones. Much depends on what the existing divisions are. I've worked with one assessment guide and report cards that span pre-K through grade 2, another for grades 3 through 6, one for grades 7 and 8, and one for grades 9 through 12. But in other districts, where the middle school spans grades 6, 7, and 8, we created one assessment guide for middle school. In the project I am currently working on, we have one guide for preschool through pre-K, one for K through grade 2, one for grades 3 through 6, and one for grades 7 through 12.

The next step is working on the assessment guides themselves. I typically work through one or two examples, showing different ways that previous guides have been written. Then we divide the language arts committee into smaller groups, sometimes adding members to ensure that each guide or report card group has sufficient representation from the grade levels. These groups work on the various elements of the guide and report cards. However, each guide starts with some sections that are common to all the guides: a brief description of the framework and its components; an acknowledgments page (very important), and a listing of the literacy attributes and non-negotiable instructional contributions, with examples of instructional contributions.

The sections following these common pages are unique to each guide or report card. The first is a mock-up of the new language arts section of the report card (elementary grades) or interim for English (secondary grades). Following that, each page corresponds to the specific attribute (or subattribute) on the report card or interim. There's a brief description of the attribute, followed by instructions for gathering evidence and for analyzing the evidence to fill out the report card (see Exhibits 9.2, 9.2a, and 9.2b).

Exhibit 9.2. Extract from Assessment Guide.

Identifies Letters, Letter Sounds

Letter Identification. Using one of the sheets provided (one sheet contains all upper- and lowercase letters; the others list upper- and lowercase separately), ask each student individually to name the letters of the alphabet (start with uppercase, then work through lowercase, using the same order of letters as is on the scoring sheet). Mark responses on the Individual Scoring Sheet with a checkmark for each correct response.

Letter Sounds. Next, ask students to give you each letter's sound, again using the same order of presentation. For letters with more than one sound (A, O, U, C, Y, I, E, G), ask the student for other sounds. You'll see that there's an upper and lower part of the boxes for these letters to mark two responses per letter.

Once a student has answered an item correctly, do not test this item again.

Finally, tally totals on the Individual Scoring Sheet then convert these to 1 to 4 using the conversion table below. Enter the results on the report card.

Note: Once a student has mastered this assessment, it is not reassessed.

If a student has not mastered letters and letter sounds by the end of the 2nd grade, continue the assessment but record results in the Comments section (beyond 2nd grade, the progress report does not have letters and letter sounds listed).

Conversion Table

	Letter ID	Sound
4	53–55	32–34
3	46–52	21–31
2	11–45	6–20
1	0–10	0–5

The process we use to share and revise the guides follows a by-now-familiar pattern: the language arts committee creates the drafts and takes them back to their buildings for informal review and suggestions. Once the final drafts are completed, they are formally shared with all the faculty and administrators in each school; then, based on this feedback, final versions are printed up.

Piloting the Assessments and Report Cards

Before finalizing the new assessments and report cards, we always pilot them. Although informal piloting has already taken place (for example, testing out rubrics, conversion tables, and scoring criteria), there's no substitute for the real thing. Too often, districts go ahead with new report cards that haven't been properly piloted and suffer the consequences later. Worse, they sometimes print ten thousand copies of multipart forms, which then obligates them to stick with the report cards for at least five years.

In some projects, we have piloted the new report cards for a year, only printing up enough copies for that year and letting parents know that's what we are doing. More recently, we have asked for volunteers across the grades to pilot the new report cards alongside the current ones. Only one or two classes at a grade level are chosen (in fact, despite the additional work involved, we had to turn down some volunteers). The parents are informed about this and asked to provide detailed feedback on the new report cards. By

Exhibit 9.2a. Letter Identification/Letter-Sounds Worksheet.

A	F	K	P	W	Z
B	H	O	J	U	
C	Y	L	Q	M	
D	N	S	X	I	
E	G	R	V	T	
a	f	k	p	w	z
b	h	o	j	u	a
c	y	l	q	m	
d	n	s	x	i	q
e	g	r	v	l	g

Exhibit 9.2b. Individual Scoring Sheet.

Letter Identification/Letter-Sound Relationships
Individual Scoring Sheet

Student_____   Year_____

Recorder_____ Teacher_____ Grade_____ School_____

Names (Upper case)				Names (Lower case)				Sounds				
1	2	3	4	1	2	3	4	1	2	3	4	
Name	Name	Name	Name	Name	Name	Name	Name	Name	Name	Name	Name	
A				a				A				
F				f				F				
K				k				K				
P				p				P				
W				w				W				
Z				z				Z				
B				b				B				
H				h				H				
O				o				O				
J				j				J				
U				u				U				
				a								
C				c				Z				
Y				y				Y				
L				l				L				
Q				q				Q				
M				m				M				
D				d				D				
N				n				N				
S				s				S				
X				x				X				
I				i				I				
E				e				E				
				q								
G				g				G				
R				r				R				
V				v				V				
T				t				T				
				g								

Key for Sound

Short [ ] Long

Key for Consonants

Hard [ ] Soft

Y Sounds:
Any 2 of these:
"y" Yellow
"i" Cry
"e" Happy

Names (Upper case)

	1	2	3	4
Max Total	26	26	26	26

Names (Lower case)

	1	2	3	4
Max Total	29	29	29	29

Sounds

	1	2	3	4
Max Total	34	34	34	34

doing it in smaller steps, we were able to pinpoint issues that needed to be addressed (for example, language that was too complicated, errors in conversion tables) before going districtwide. Parents were grateful to be included in the process, especially when they realized that their input would be taken seriously. In future projects, this is the approach I will routinely recommend. I thought that having teachers fill out two sets of report cards would be strenuously resisted, but it wasn't, and one of the side benefits was that both teachers and parents could see how much better the new report cards were than the old ones. Of course, had they not been, the outcome might have been different. In any event, seeking input from parents (not just through the PTA but parents drawn from across the grades) is a critical step. After all, it's the parents for whom the report card was primarily designed.

Creating Parent Guides

In addition to involving parents in piloting revised report cards and holding informational meetings with them, creating a parent guide is a worthwhile task. I have only done this once thus far, but having done it, I will encourage it in all future projects.

In the guide we created for parents in Harrison, New York (see Exhibit 9.3), we took a page or two to describe the district's new language arts philosophy and then described each of the attributes and what parents should expect to see going on in their child's classroom to acquire that attribute. We also laid out the most important contributions parents could make. In the second half of the guide, we walked parents through the report card, explaining how it worked and what the scores on each of the attributes meant. It's too early to assess the full impact of this guide, but thus far the reaction from parents has been very positive.

One aspect of this guide that I am hoping will be added in future versions is to add, for each attribute, what students themselves can contribute so that the guide articulates the contributions we expect from teachers, parents, and students.

Exhibit 9.3. Extract from Parent Guide.

Reading

Our reading attributes–what we want a student to look like as a reader and what we want him/her to have experienced–reflect our commitment to engaging students in and achieving excellence in reading. There are three major reading attributes:

Decodes fluently

Understands what is read

Reads widely

In the following sections, each of these attributes is listed and explained.

Decodes Fluently

By decoding fluently, we mean that a student:

- is able to decode continuous text at an appropriate level, using appropriate reading strategies.
- understands basic conventions of print (that text flows from top to bottom, left to right; what simple punctuation marks are; one-to-one correspondence between text and oral reading, etc.)
- recognizes upper and lower case letters of the alphabet.
- demonstrates phonemic awareness.
- knows simple letter-sound relationships.
- recognizes sight words.
- has a basic/literal understanding of text.

We expect that decoding fluency will be attained by almost all students at the end of second grade. However, a student who doesn't yet decode fluently will continue to receive instructional support in grade 3 or beyond.

Why is decoding fluently important?

If students' decoding abilities are not fluent, they will not be able to focus their full attention on the meaning of the texts they are reading, nor will they find reading a pleasurable and satisfying activity. On the other hand, decoding is only one aspect of reading and it is a co-requisite, not a prerequisite, for successful reading comprehension.

What does it mean to decode fluently?

A reader decodes fluently when he or she can easily pronounce words that are frequently encountered in text (sight words) and uncommon or new words.

What should you expect to see your child engaged in and being taught?

- Basic conventions of print (left-to-right progression, return sweep, one-to-one correspondence, etc.) are modeled, taught, and practiced.
- Children are immersed in a print-rich environment.
- Appropriate direct instruction is provided in decoding skills.
- Strategies for fluent decoding are modeled, taught, and practiced.

How can you support your child's growth toward this attribute?

- Read aloud daily to your child and, when appropriate, have your child read or find known words.
- Play word and letter games.
- Read alphabet books.
- Find teachable moments to introduce or reinforce letters, letter-sounds, and words as they are encountered in books and in the environment.
- Share in the reading of books brought home from school by your child.
- Ask your child's teacher for specific recommendations.

Going Beyond the Language Arts Committee

Everything that I have discussed thus far pertains to getting an attributes framework in place. Of course, that's only half the story. The other half is all about making it live and breathe in each and every classroom.

I am convinced that once the assessments and report cards are in place, implementation of the non-negotiables and instructional activities will not be far behind. I vividly recall, in a first-grade classroom in Gilbertsville-Mt. Upton, a first-year teacher was being mentored into the attributes framework there. One day, I was in her classroom, and I noticed that she had one of the children sitting beside her; he was reading a passage from a book. As I watched, the teacher was coaching him on how to differentiate between two characters in the book, as he read the dialogue between them. She read the lines with expression and then asked the child to copy her. After a few minutes, a great big grin came over his face. "I got it!" he exclaimed. "Are you ready to read to the class?" she asked. And read to the class he did, with expression and different voices for the two characters. Later, I asked the teacher about this episode. "Well," she said, "I knew I had to report on each child's ability to read with expression, and I knew if I didn't do some coaching, it wouldn't happen. I did, and as you saw, it worked. I still have a lot to learn, but if Joey can do it, so can the other struggling readers."

I am more convinced, however, that full implementation of an attributes framework is going to come about not just because teachers are held accountable for them but because they have made them part of their own literacy philosophy and an integral part of their classroom day.

There are several key components of making the framework a self-sustaining enterprise. One is to attend to areas of concern that are either expressed by faculty and staff or that turn up as issues in the assessment data. For example, if teachers find that administering the DRA produces erratic levels over time or takes an inordinate amount of time, these concerns need to be aired and solutions found. Or if an analysis of the assessment data shows continuing weakness in students' understanding of informational text, this needs to become the subject of discussion at faculty meetings. Especially in the initial years of implementation, there will be key issues that merit intensive professional development. One of these, I suspect, will be seriously bumping up the amount and quality of students' experiences with poetry across the grades. Another will probably be how best to improve the attention paid to "big ideas." Refining and improving assessment is bound to be an issue, especially in literacy areas that traditionally have been neglected on report cards ("reads widely" comes to mind immediately). In fact, professional development (for example, through study groups, teachers-as-readers, consultants, literacy coaches, conference attendance and presentations) is a critical vehicle for teachers and administrators to keep up-to-date and to share professional knowledge.

Another, as I have mentioned before, is for supervisors to keep the framework in mind as they observe teachers and as they engage teachers in grade-level or subject-area discussions.

A third is to make sure that new faculty joining the district are properly trained in the district's policies and procedures for implementing the non-negotiables through appropriate instructional activities, especially that they understand the philosophy and practice of assessing literacy progress.

Finally, a framework that doesn't grow is a framework that's dying. As new understandings about literacy teaching become available and as student populations change, the framework has to incorporate what's best in the professional literature and accommodate to shifts in what students bring with them to school. If you've been a teacher for any length of time, you've had to adapt to changes in students, in the school and community, and in the society at large. An attributes framework must also change to meet these new challenges.

Summary

When I first started working with school districts, I was naïve about how to implement an attributes approach, mostly because I had yet to figure out all of its components. But even when I had the framework under control, I had very little idea about how it should be implemented, or indeed whether it could be. I remember thinking that was the district's responsibility.

Over the years, as the framework itself resonated more with teachers and administrators, several districts asked me to help them put it into practice, and that initiated a series of projects that led ultimately to me being able to write this chapter.

I think the key to successful implementation lies in being realistic about how long it will take, sticking with it, paying close attention to teachers' and administrators' concerns, building on what teachers already know and do, and being willing to tolerate mistakes and ambiguity until the routines become part of the fabric of each and every classroom. Just as we try to help students become self-sustaining and independent, we need to do likewise with teachers. The process of handing over the responsibility and ownership of an attributes approach needs to begin on the first day of implementation.

In the process of working with schools over many years to implement an attributes approach, I have slowly (and painfully) gained some insights about the process, and in the final chapter, I want to reflect on what I think seems to work well, and what challenges still lie ahead.

10

THE PROMISE AND CHALLENGE OF LITERACY REFORM

For two years, after graduating from Trinity College, Dublin, I taught remedial English in a private secondary school in Somerset, England. The chair of my department was Len Smith, and one of the first things he did was to introduce me to the work of James Moffett—specifically, his *Teaching the Universe of Discourse* (1967). Not long afterward, Len asked me to write a chapter in a book he had written on a spiraling English curriculum (Smith 1972). I think that's when I started the long journey that culminates in the present volume. What Moffett and Smith challenged me to think about was the big picture of language arts at a time when I was immersed only in the minutiae of remedial reading.

As I look back on nearly thirty years of training literacy teachers and doctoral students, and relentlessly pursuing the big picture of language arts, there are a number of lessons that I've learned that I'd like to share in this final chapter; some of them make me optimistic that the work we have accomplished is worth the effort, and some leave me with nagging doubts.

Keep It Simple, and Say It Often

If you've been following the saga of No Child Left Behind over the past few years, you will have noticed how effectively the Bush administration has used simple language to frame and control the public's definition of literacy, as well as their willingness to buy into the idea that if only schools used "scientifically based" reading programs, children wouldn't be left behind. Whatever one thinks about NCLB, you have to admire the effectiveness of the campaign, brought about in large measure through consistent and persistent repetitions of simple messages, even when countered by hard evidence to the contrary or charges of malfeasance from the inspector general's office. The idea that the "faddish" Whole Language movement crippled a generation of readers and that explicit instruction in phonics is the only way to remedy the damage created by "liberal" education professors has undoubtedly taken hold among parents, legislators, state departments of education, and many educators, too. Saying simple things over and over again turns out to be very persuasive, especially in an environment like literacy, where things that most people can do without even thinking about them, like reading, are in fact extremely complex processes.

One lesson I've learned from my work with schools is that although developing children's literacy (in its broadest sense) is very complex, both in terms of what that actually means and in terms of how to make it happen, you have to communicate the process of reform in simple terms. This is, of course, the precise opposite of the way most researchers and scholars behave. And sure enough, although one can bring the university into schools, if one complicates literacy learning and teaching too much, the reforms probably won't last. This is not a criticism of the intelligence of school educators but a recognition that simplicity is more likely to be effective. Another way of thinking about this is a theory-practice continuum, where theory is, by definition, complicated and needs to be simplified if it is to prevail in a school setting.

The other lesson I've learned is that however clearly I see the big picture or the direction in which I think a district might be headed, that vision is not likely to be immediately shared or understood by participants. In some of the early projects, I think I became impatient because I could see where we were going and couldn't understand why others were having difficulty. I also thought that if I explained things once and explained clearly, they would understand. It never occurred to me that some of the resistance I encountered stemmed from not fully understanding rather than understanding clearly and not liking where we were going. In more recent projects, I find myself doing what the Bush administration does, which is to present the framework in much simpler terms than I used to and then repeatedly connect everything back to that framework. Here's an example.

The further away from articulating literacy attributes you get, the more likely you are to focus on the task at hand and forget that all aspects of the framework need to be driven by the attributes. So when creating appropriate literacy assessments, it's easy to forget that they have to be tied directly to the attributes. But unless someone (typically me) continually reminds committee members to do this, assessments will quickly wander away from the attributes and back to assessing what teachers typically teach. Unless the ties are reconnected, it only takes a few working sessions and the entire assessment phase is out of kilter with the attributes. This can, of course, arise from a deliberate attempt to sabotage the process (for example, trying to return to assessing only decoding skills in reading), but most frequently, it's not malicious or intentional at all. Yet from a consultant's perspective, you wonder why it strayed in the first place.

The Inevitability Factor

Some time ago, I read Robert McNeill's wonderful book, *Wordstruck* (MacNeil 1989), in which he reminisced on his own fascination with words and language and the origins of this fascination in his early home and school life, growing up in Nova Scotia. The book resonated with me, not just because I have a similar interest in language but because the schools he attended in Canada in the 1930s had exactly the same educational philosophy and instructional practices as the schools I attended as a child in the 1950s. But his school had pretty much the same approach in the 1840s! True, the high school I attended now has a much more modern curriculum, but serious reforms really didn't take place until the early 1970s.

If there's one thing that characterizes American public education, it's that education has undergone huge numbers of reforms; recently, the pace has been quickening to the point where one reform begins before the last one is barely out of the wrapper.

And it isn't just reforms that schools themselves initiate. Many times, schools are simply reacting to mandates created by state departments of education, the federal government (especially since 2001), legislators, and the like. I sometimes think that whenever governments or society can't solve a social issue, they insist on schools solving it, typically through programs or initiatives that barely scratch the surface of the problem yet occupy valuable learning time and increasingly fractionate the school day to the point where legislators must recommend lengthening the school day to accommodate all the mandates. Does the D.A.R.E. program (shown by scientific studies not to be effective, according to a General Accounting Office (GAO) report (Kanoff 2003)), and Character Education come to mind as examples? Or one of my favorites, a bill introduced to the New York State assembly a few years ago by a local politician, to require ninety minutes of explicit phonics instruction a day in every elementary grade! (It was dead on arrival in the assembly.)

In this environment, I don't wonder that teachers are skeptical about any new initiative, and I'm no longer surprised when teachers tell me that what I'm proposing is simply another in a long string of initiatives that their district will abandon within a year or so when the next one comes along to replace it.

Yet it amazes me how quickly this changes when a project respects what has gone before, deals with the practicalities of expectations, instruction, and assessment, and shows even the slightest signs of being carried through. And the further it progresses, the more what I call the inevitability factor kicks in. Once teachers realize it is going to happen, they are more willing to engage in the process, and the more they do that, the more they own the reforms being carried out. So an important lesson here is that if a district really does want to make a lasting reform, all they need to do is stick with it, and the very fact of staying with it actually makes it happen. Of course, this principle works just as well with a reform that is poorly conceived as one that is well thought out.

The other thing that happens is that as a reform gets more traction, more of the teaching and administrative staff buy into it, even those who initially opposed it. However, I've noticed a difference between elementary and secondary teachers in this regard. Elementary teachers often say yes to initiatives they will have difficulty in implementing, while many middle and high school teachers just say no at the outset. I've learned not to be too excited, either by elementary teachers' initial enthusiasm or secondary teachers' initial apathy.

Opposing Points of View

When I first came to the United States, I was trained in Orton-Gillingham and was completely convinced (and wrote an article in the *Washington Post* to that effect) that if only O-G was used in all schools, there would be no dyslexics anymore. Now, as I've broadened my view of literacy, I frequently encounter students and teachers who tell me all about this wonderful new approach called Orton-Gillingham that, if everyone used, would rid schools of struggling students. I smile.

I am now hugely conflicted as I work on a project that promotes what I think is a balanced approach to literacy and opposes some of what I consider to be narrow conceptions of literacy. This has become particularly troubling in the past few years, as more educators fall in line with the Bush administration's literacy ideology (I would have loved that in the early 1970s) and are adamant that if an approach doesn't have "replicable scientific evidence" to support it, the district shouldn't be using it. But equally, I have difficulties translating or promoting some of the principles of critical literacy (see Chapter Two) that are so important to my colleagues at the university. Whenever I have tried to incorporate them into the attributes framework, they are well received initially but don't survive the second or third round of revisions, even when I'm actively promoting them.

I wonder if the reason is that most teachers are quite a bit more conservative in their role as school educators than they are as university graduate students (and definitely less progressive than their professors), or is it that the professors haven't worked out in sufficient detail what their theoretical principles would look like in a regular public school setting? Perhaps a bit of both. I do notice that some of my colleagues both within my own School of Education and those from other universities who have worked extensively with schools, tend to gravitate to schools whose prevailing philosophies are akin to theirs—or at least they work with colleagues within schools who share common understandings. In my situation, I tend to work with schools that are looking for assistance with raising test scores, narrowing the achievement gap, rethinking the big picture of language arts, or simply trying to balance their K–12 language arts programs. So I tend to work with districts that aren't as predisposed to countercultural educational ideologies.

However, I've been able to represent and privilege a range of different views of literacy in two important ways. One is that in articulating attributes, we deliberately avoid defining them as simply skills (the typical manner in which language arts curricula are defined); the initial conversations with faculty and staff about what's important about literacy always include the full range of perspectives. But more important, the attributes framework does not prescribe a particular set of instructional philosophies; rather, it challenges teachers to provide whatever instruction (intentional, incidental), activities, and experiences that best lead toward the literacy attributes. Because the criterion for success is measured not in terms of adherence to a specific philosophy but rather accomplishing literacy outcomes, the framework cannot be criticized for being instructionally lopsided. But it can be criticized for adopting a particular set of literacy expectations. And worse than that, if everything from pre-K through grade 12 is focused on those expectations, getting them wrong is potentially disastrous. At least in the muddled, haphazard language arts programs that characterize most schools, students are likely to encounter the full range of literacy ideologies by the time they graduate. So which is better? Spending time making an informed decision to define literacy outcomes and then relating everything to those, or adopting a free-market approach where students accidentally bump into different philosophical experiences?

For me, the big worry is that ten years from now, when someone proposes an entirely different set of literacy outcomes for schools, the outcomes I have so diligently pursued will no longer be relevant. I keep thinking back to those halcyon days with Orton-Gillingham, convinced that I had the answers. At least now I know I don't, but I see others following in my footsteps who are as convinced that they do as I was.

The other thing about opposing points of view that I've learned over the course of these projects is that when people disagree with you, it forces you to think more deeply than when they agree with you. In fact, I think I learn the most when I'm arguing or being argued with. Sadly, these days we don't argue enough about things that matter to us, and arguments in schools are often avoided for fear of offending colleagues, or worse, having to defend a point of view. We tend to avoid confrontation so much that we lose the ability to engage in civil discourse, and that leads to even less discussion. One of the hardest tasks for me as a consultant is to get educators to engage in serious and thoughtful discussion about the issues we need to resolve.

The other thing I've noticed is how reluctant educators are to do their homework. Too easily, they are swayed by colleagues, salespeople, consultants, the Internet, and the lighter education journals. I'm not suggesting that they ought only to be reading the heaviest professional journals, but I find frequently that views expressed in meetings are often shallow and unexamined. And worse than that, when views are put forward that are both well informed and well balanced, those who express them are sometimes regarded as arrogant and overbearing.

In my own work with schools (as with my graduate classes), I have always tried to engage educators in different points of view. This has often gotten me into trouble, when I'm perceived as being too "fair" or as giving credence to points of view the district opposes. But my goal is not to end up with a wishy-washy approach that gives lip service to all perspectives in an attempt to offend no one. Rather, it's a firmly held belief in taking different points of view seriously, learning where others are coming from (by reading their accounts rather than what others think of them), and taking from them ideas that can actually strengthen the district's literacy philosophy. Whenever you take seriously someone else's perspective, you gain respect yourself. You don't have to agree with them, and you don't have to adopt their approach, but just taking the time to listen often results in improving your approach and frequently results in their acquiescing in it. This is not easy to do, and I've failed on numerous occasions, but it always has good results when it's done.

There's a political lesson to be learned here. If you advocate or initiate a reform that relies on the inevitability factor to succeed (we all agree on a single approach and implement it in a determined manner, allowing little or no dissent), then you'll probably achieve what you set out to accomplish. How long that reform lasts depends on whether it truly becomes part of the fabric of every classroom and whether those who initiated it stay on to live it through. Of course, the reforms equally might not yield desired results, however enthusiastically they are embraced by the school community. But I think reforms work better in the long run if they develop a philosophy that encourages opposing points of view at all stages of the reforms. The trick is not to let opposing points of view result in diluting the chosen philosophy to the point where it becomes the lowest common denominator but rather to continually engage the dominant philosophy with different points of view, so that it (1) respects different and legitimate perspectives and (2) modifies its approach when compelling arguments or evidence is justified. So the dominant philosophy is continually examined and updated, rather than thrown out as soon as something else comes down the pike.

There are, of course, other ways to deal with opposing views. In a larger district, one could always create magnet schools that have "purer" versions of educational philosophies than are possible with a single approach. However, in districts where I have initially been excited to see these carried out, I've noticed that they are rarely "pure" and rarely last that long; they are constantly battered by critics who complain, not without cause, that different approaches within the same district are biased, inconsistent, and unfair to students. Sadly, the response to these critics is to retreat from the philosophies and return to the bland, don't-offend-anyone approach that characterizes most American public schools. No wonder so many parents want vouchers and charter schools! And the more they succeed in getting them, the more bland the schools that remain become.

Sustainability

Marie Clay once said that it takes about ten years to initiate and implement any serious educational reform, and I have always been in awe of what she and her colleagues accomplished in New Zealand with Reading Recovery. I've also been hugely saddened that Reading Recovery has recently become so vilified by the Bush administration—an odd fate for an approach that is so structured, thorough, and direct in its instructional methods. (In an ironic reversal just after Marie Clay's passing, Reading Recovery was designated by the U.S. Department of Education as the only approach to beginning reading that has strong evidence of a positive impact on general reading achievement, with no contrary findings). So I've never shied away from the notion that a fundamental reform of K–12 language arts would take a decade to carry out. But America isn't New Zealand (and probably New Zealand today isn't the New Zealand of yesteryear, either), and increasingly I've observed that in almost every sphere of American life, *long term* is no longer part of anyone's vocabulary. School districts are no exception, with shortened tenure of top administrators, annual high-stakes testing, political interference, to name just a few of the factors that mitigate against long-range planning. Perhaps Alan Toffler was right in saying that the world is changing at an ever-increasing rate, so what's the point of looking too far beyond the horizon, only to be proved wrong about where the future lies? Also, our own lives have become so busy and occupied that we can barely deal with what has to be done this week, let alone next year and beyond. No wonder that one of the most popular—and probably necessary—topics for teacher workshops is how to handle stress!

So there's a tension between language arts reforms that demand sustained amounts of time to implement and districts' unwillingness to engage in long-term reforms. At the same time, the pressure to produce short-term results makes long-term investments almost foolhardy. Taken together, it should come as no surprise that districts willingly engage in short-term projects and, while professing interest in the long term, don't actually follow through with long-term projects. Even if they could, frequent changes in top administrators make it almost impossible to do so.

One of the lessons I've learned from this is that if you want to engage in long-term reforms, you need to make them as short term as possible, because in most districts, the energy and commitment that will be devoted to your reforms will almost certainly flag after a year or so, despite what is said at the outset. In my early projects, I wasn't able to proceed any faster, because I simply didn't know enough about how to rethink all the components of a K–12 language arts program. For example, I knew how to develop simple and clear literacy expectations but wasn't at all sure how to implement these in classrooms that used a variety of instructional approaches, and I didn't have a clue about how to keep track of student progress toward the expectations. Anyway, it would take up to a year of fairly intensive work just to articulate the literacy attributes, so we'd run out of time and commitment before we even started rethinking the curriculum. One of the reasons I initially recommended reforming the assessments immediately after the attributes was because I knew that revised report cards would drive changes in the curriculum (if you insist that teachers report on students' ability to read with expression, they will attend to expressive reading in their classroom, as I pointed out in Chapter Seven). Later, when I'd figured out how to do the assessments, the process of articulating literacy attributes and assessments could be done quickly enough to permit working on the instructional contributions as well as—and in some cases, prior to—the assessments.

However, even if the basic components of language arts reforms could be speeded up, Marie Clay's warning about how long it takes to transform the reforms into standard practices still holds true. So how can this be done?

When I look at some of the reforms that I admire so much in the professional literature, especially those that if you now went back to the schools they were initiated in, you'd see no trace of them. They seem to depend on the strong leadership of consultants or leaders within the schools. Sometimes teachers are so empowered by the reforms that they leave and become consultants and authors themselves—great for them personally but perhaps not terribly sustaining for the district they abandoned! Of course, the ones perhaps most enlightened by these projects are the consultants. I know that most of what I have learned about how to reform K–12 language arts has come from working with so many talented teachers, specialists, and administrators over the years, and I am sure I have benefited a great deal more than some of the districts with whom I consulted. But in recent projects, especially now that the timeframe for working with a district has been shortened so much, I've given a lot more attention to the notion of sustainability and how it can be nurtured.

First, sustainability needs to be defined less in terms of fully implementing an external consultant's vision of language arts reform, no matter how well that is articulated, and more in terms of ownership by those who inhabit the school buildings. In other words, a reform can be considered successful only if the ownership passes from consultant to teachers, such that it no longer belongs to an outsider. You'll notice that I use the term *teachers* here, not administrators. I do so for an important reason. Think about the average tenure of teachers versus administrators, and you'll see why it's the teachers who need to own the reforms, not the administrators. Administrators can help or hurt reforms, but they rarely see them through even for the time it takes for a kindergartner to graduate from high school, let alone for three or four generations of students! When I think about this, it's true of higher education, too. In my tenure at the University at Albany, I've seen five deans of the School of Education and at least four presidents. Each one has had different management styles, different strategic visions, and different priorities. I used to laugh when deans or presidents asked us to create long-range plans—stretching five years into the future, even more—when I knew perfectly well that the only realistic plan was the one that covered the present and next year ahead. Yet within our department, we have faculty who have been here for twenty-plus years. If anyone is to "own" the curriculum, it needs to be those who have the greatest stake in it and will be around for the longest time to carry it out.

Second, sustainability inevitably implies further changes. Many years ago, I helped implement a literature-based K–7 language arts program in a rural, upstate New York school. We changed the entire language arts program from a reading subskills basal reading series by implementing content-rich themes across the grades. It was not easy, and it took a long time. The proof that ownership was transferred to the teachers came later, as each superintendent tried—and failed—to unravel it. In fact, only in the past two years has it finally been unraveled, and even now, the Board of Education is beginning to think it should have been left alone. But although I regard this project as a viable example of sustainability, I also worry that the seeds of its destruction were planted quite early on. I was expecting that most of the themes, which were largely created by the reading teacher and myself, would eventually be abandoned in favor of newer themes that individual teachers would develop on their own as they became more invested in the approach and able to modify or replace them with new-found knowledge and experience. This didn't happen, and many of the themes that I would have replaced years ago have become rather routine and dated, except, of course, there are no themes any more, having been replaced by a basal reading series. But to be fair, the themes weren't replaced because they were no longer effective; they were let go because the superintendent felt that a basal series would offer a more "consistent" language arts curriculum.

Finally, I think I am now comfortable with the idea that sustainability may not, in itself, be the most important principle, because it cannot be guaranteed and increasingly isn't even desired. From a consultant's perspective, just the fact that you have offered some different and thoughtful ways of defining expectations, curriculum, and assessment that resonate with teachers and administrators and lead to changes they can make in their own classrooms, makes the contribution worthwhile. If you can help a school or district accomplish its own literacy goals in a more efficient and satisfactory way, that is a significant contribution. And then, very occasionally, you work with a district that is willing to take a risk and invest in reforms over as long as a decade, and you help change—for a significant period of time—the entire infrastructure of a K–12 language arts program. It is only in projects of this kind, where all the elements of a K–12 language arts program—theory, pedagogy, goal setting, curriculum, organization, assessment, data analysis, and of course politics—have to be understood and integrated. This is easier in a small district or in a single school and much harder in larger districts that serve greater percentages of minority students. Yet the lessons learned in all these situations are invaluable and can, in turn, be useful to others as they face similar challenges. Indeed, if there are any useful insights to be gained from this book, the chances are they came from attempting to solve problems in one of the many projects I have been engaged in over the past twenty-five years.

The Big Picture

I'm not sure how this happened, and I certainly didn't set out to accomplish it, but I have been very fortunate over the years to have spent time in classrooms and schools that serve infants and toddlers at one end of the spectrum and graduate students at the other. I am as comfortable in a pre-K classroom sitting in a chair designed to accommodate a very small posterior as I am wedged into one of those desk chairs in a twelfth-grade classroom. And I'm well used to teaching graduate classes at the university. At first, I was intimidated in grade levels where I'd never taught but eventually became familiar with their routines and curriculum, so that now I have a very broad set of experiences on which to draw. Once districts realized that I had this experience, they became more interested in my working across levels rather than just at one level, and as these projects continued, I became much more knowledgeable about literacy issues from pre-K through twelfth grade. At the same time, I served as an evaluator for a local Even Start program and began to wonder if an attributes framework would work with much younger children (birth through pre-K). Not only has that proved to be workable within Even Start, it has also led to thinking about the entire span from birth through twelfth grade. As luck would have it, I am now engaged in a multiyear project with one of the only public school districts in New York State that has taken on the responsibility of educating children as young as infants.

These experiences have led inevitably to having a much broader view of literacy than might have been possible had I stayed focused on just elementary school. It also has made me conscious of the inevitable narrowness of most teachers' notions about literacy, given that they spend most of their time with a single grade level. I often say to teachers that we need each other—they clearly know more about a given grade level than I will ever grasp, but I know more about the literacy experiences that their students will have from birth through twelfth grade. That broad perspective is invaluable because it allows connections to be made between the earliest grades and the later ones that teachers in those grades typically don't, and perhaps cannot, make.

One example: I spent some time in a rural school in upstate New York and one day found myself in a kindergarten classroom. I was not having much fun, because the teacher in this room had one of those mannerisms—a high-pitched, patronizing voice, you know what I mean—that made me wince each time she used it to move the children from one area to another. Anyway, just as I was thinking about how to leave the room, she drew the children into a circle on the rug and proceeded to pull out a copy of the *Albany Times-Union*. She had clearly done this before. She pointed to the front page and said to the children, "Here's someone cutting a ribbon outside a building. I wonder who it is and why he's doing that." One of the children said, "It's the president." The teacher said, "No, actually it isn't, but that's a good guess; it's someone important" and then went on to explain it was the governor, and he was opening a new wing of a hospital. She then turned to the Op-Ed page, reminding the children that on this page, the newspaper said what it thought about things and where people wrote letters about things they were thinking. She picked a letter written by someone about trapping—a topic of intense interest to these rural children—and read it aloud, then engaged the children in a conversation about it. Later, as she turned the pages, a child exclaimed, "There's a story about a sofa!"

"No," the teacher smiled. "It's an advertisement for a sofa! How much do you think a sofa costs?"

Later, I asked the teacher how often she did this, and it turns out just five minutes a day, almost every day. Why did she do it?

She felt that children needed to know more about newspapers, and this was a quick and easy way to do it. The very next week, I was in a suburban school, talking to elementary teachers about nonfiction reading and writing. I suggested they should be having children read the newspaper. A fifth-grade teacher was quick to complain. "I've asked the district to supply multiple copies of newspapers, and they refused. So we just do one newspaper unit later in the year, and that's enough." I let it go, but I couldn't help thinking about the kindergarten teacher with her supercilious voice, making such good contributions to children's knowledge of newspapers, but even more important, to their knowledge of the world. And since then, I've realized that one can articulate a myriad ways in which contributions can be made in early grades, even before coming to school, that lay down foundational knowledge in little encounters that eventually build up into understandings of really big ideas. In fact, we'll never be able to articulate a birth-through-twelfth-grade language arts curriculum unless we can grasp the bigger picture.

Paths Not Yet Taken

Finally, I want to discuss some issues that have yet to be resolved in an attributes approach. Perhaps someone out there has already thought these through, and all I need to do is find them and incorporate their solutions. The issues are (1) defining literacy across the curriculum and (2) integrating an attributes approach with the rest of the school curriculum.

Introducing Literacy Across the Curriculum. A question always arises in the language arts projects: How can we involve teachers of other subjects, given that their content areas are heavily dependent on language processes? Indeed they are. But I have always run into roadblocks when I try to engage content-area teachers in our projects, mostly because the school administrators restrict our focus to language arts and English teachers. They do this typically not for malicious reasons, they want to get the language arts programs under control before tackling literacy across the curriculum. However, the result is always the same: we rarely get to work across subject areas. I have made some dents in this barrier by insisting during a language arts audit that I interview teachers across subject areas, and these have yielded important insights about both the problem and potential solutions. The main issue is one of compartmentalization, especially in the upper-elementary, middle, and high schools, where students are taught in separate classes. But this also stretches down into the elementary grades, where "specials" often achieve the same separation of language arts and content areas. And I have to acknowledge that, even here, there are legitimate reasons for fractionating the curriculum, if only to provide weary elementary teachers with a break for planning or grabbing something to eat!

The role of language arts in subject areas is critical, and I very much regret not yet having had a chance to integrate literacy across the curriculum into the projects in substantial ways. It's a path I've started along but not traveled far enough.

In the literacy field, the traditional perspective is that content-area teachers should be reading teachers, but this is too narrow a conception of literacy across the curriculum. If one adopts a definition of literacy that embraces reading, writing, listening, speaking, viewing, and representing, as well as knowledge of the world, then it becomes obvious that language arts has much to contribute to content areas, and content areas have much to contribute to language arts. In fact, in order to maximize students' growth toward the literacy attributes, these contributions are pivotal.

Second, it's important to remember that language arts are not themselves subject areas, although sometimes as I wander through classrooms, many teachers treat them as such. The relationship between language arts and subject areas should be that language provides the processes by which content is *acquired* (reading, listening, viewing) and by which understandings about the content are *communicated* (writing, speaking, representing). The subject areas are mostly about knowledge of the world. But they also have their own unique ways of representing their particular knowledge. Let me give a couple of examples. In order for students to read and comprehend scientific material, they have to understand that books and articles that explore scientific topics are generally written in logical, nonfiction prose and that making sense of the content of these materials requires applying a much more logical set of reading strategies than, say, trying to make sense of a Shakespearean sonnet. It isn't just the vocabulary and the syntax; it's also the entire way in which topics are approached and framed by writers. Making sense of metamorphosis in a science textbook requires quite different strategies than making sense of a literary work on the same topic, like Kafka's "Metamorphosis." And when it comes to communicating understanding in subject areas, look at the difference between the conventions of writing up a scientific experiment, a poem, a critical analysis of a painting or a musical performance, a description of a historical event, or an interpretation of a character in a novel. In both receptive and expressive uses of language in subject areas, students not only acquire important content knowledge; they also get to learn and use language strategies across all components of language arts.

So the benefits of these engagements across the curriculum accrue to both language arts and subject areas. Sadly, this is not typically what I find in schools. Mostly, I hear repeated complaints by science teachers that their students can't write in complete sentences and their spelling is atrocious. However, occasionally I come across a science teacher who gets the point of understanding and communicating like a scientist and provides students with both experiences and coaching in how to accomplish this. It's not that writing in complete sentences and spelling aren't important; it's that there's a more important set of skills and strategies that is typically neglected.

One of the worst things we can do to music and art teachers is insist that they act like reading and writing teachers. I have seen this happen so frequently in schools that I now tackle it head-on.

One of the few places where viewing and representing are a perfect fit is in the art room; similarly, listening and speaking (or more precisely, speaking in the form of singing) are ideally matched to music classes. To increase the amount of reading and writing in these classrooms at the expense of viewing, representing, listening, and speaking is to completely misunderstand the mutual contributions: viewing and representing are the primary language processes in art; listening and singing are the primary language processes in music. Think about the student who struggles with textual processing but thrives on visual. In the very area where visual processing is paramount (art), this student has to rely primarily on textual processing? It makes no sense for the art teacher, no sense for the content, and no sense for the student. Yet, I have seen, even recently, art teachers forced by their districts to make reading and writing the primary processes in their art classes.

I take it as a given that the primary purpose of teaching content areas is to have students deepen and extend their understanding of the particular content. So, when working with content-area teachers, I always try to emphasize this, and I acknowledge their content-area expertise (I have to, given how lacking I am in most of these areas!). But I then point out how much they can contribute to their students' content-area learning by embracing the language processes that figure most prominently in their subject. So exposing students to the ways in which knowledge is structured, ways in which knowledge is expressed in written, spoken, and representational forms, as well as ways in which ideas are thought about, gives students experiences that build the "schemas" embedded in the content. Teachers can also demonstrate their own strategies for making sense of what's read or observed or listened to. These instructional strategies are not necessarily what first come to mind when content-area teachers think about literacy across the curriculum, but once introduced to this perspective, they readily gravitate toward it.

The moment one takes seriously the contribution of subject areas to students' literacy development, the issue of the contribution of subject-area teachers to the assessment of students' progress toward literacy attributes comes up. This is a challenge I have yet to master. In the few instances where I have worked with content-area teachers to address this problem, I have discovered both promise and challenge. The promise is that when language arts and content-area teachers both have to assess students' understanding, say, of informational text, two things happen. One is that it fosters thoughtful conversation among teachers about individual students' understanding of nonfiction texts across subject areas. These frequently reveal that students have much better understanding of nonfiction material in some subjects than in others—in other words, not all nonfiction text is alike. The other thing that happens is that in discussing student work, teachers come to understand the real differences between reading in literature, science, social studies, math, technology, art, and music. These, incidentally, are differences that students encounter every day, as they move between classes—in one class, they need to employ one set of strategies to figure out the changes taking place in a character in a novel; the next class, they have to convert a verbal problem into mathematical formulae; in the next, they are asked to critique a sculpture or painting. Their teachers have neither need nor reason to undertake these switches but when forced to examine student work across disciplines, they begin to understand what their students have to work through on a daily basis. This is challenging even for better students; imagine what it's like for struggling learners!

The pragmatic challenge for me in this situation is that the typical report card does not easily allow for multiple, combined perspectives on students' literacy progress. So reporting on a student's understanding of nonfiction text ideally would draw evidence from all classes in which the student engaged in different kinds of nonfiction material. Although this works fairly well in self-contained classrooms in the very early grades, it becomes increasingly harder as subject areas are departmentalized. Yet the need to incorporate multiple perspectives becomes increasingly more important as literacy becomes spread across the curriculum.

Integrating a Literacy Attributes Approach with the Rest of the Curriculum. At first blush, this looks like the same topic as "literacy across the curriculum," but it isn't. This unfinished business is all about fitting a literacy attributes approach into the entire school curriculum.

One of the problems with reforms is that they tend to focus on one area of the curriculum and, by putting resources and time into that area, are often able to make significant progress in implementing new instructional strategies and producing measurable results. What I've noticed, however, is that these reforms often carve out more time in the school day than previously allocated, resulting in less time being devoted to something else. I have recently witnessed in schools a huge increase in time devoted to explicit teaching of decoding skills, at the expense of engaging children in real literature. I have also seen writing workshops implemented in schools that occupy an hour or more a day, squeezing out science and social studies. Fine for writing; not so good for content-area learning!

Until phonics and phonemic awareness took center stage, the buzz-word in language arts was *balanced literacy*. So we should expect a reasonable balance between all components of language arts, such that if a consultant recommended devoting an hour a day to writing workshop, the response would be that this would create an imbalance in language arts. But that's not typically what happens, because the district is so focused on improving writing that spending this amount of time on it is considered appropriate, and they don't even think of the consequences of this allocation in terms of other aspects of language arts. Of course, the term *balanced literacy* itself is most frequently associated with Fountas and Pinnell's "guided reading," which focuses mostly on reading, with some attention to writing. The other language arts (listening, speaking, viewing, representing) are rarely treated as important components of balanced literacy.

So the challenge here is how to incorporate an attributes approach into the whole school curriculum. I would offer several ways to do this. One might be to reorganize the entire school curriculum around attributes, so that each subject area had its own few, critical attributes and expectations for learners across the grades. Several districts I have worked with have been intrigued by this idea, but I know of none that have pursued it to the extent of the literacy attributes. This wouldn't be difficult to accomplish, especially in content areas that already have identified the most important understandings ("essential questions") of a discipline. Subject-area teachers who are used to seeing "Pays Attention in Class" and "Understands Concepts" as the only two items in science and social studies are envious of the way we have articulated literacy attributes on the report card, but there's generally little support for extending the idea across the curriculum. I think the idea has merit, in large measure because subject areas traditionally have suffered from the same lack of focus and clarity of expectations as literacy has. On the other hand, it would be a major undertaking for any district, especially those that already have heavily invested in different kinds of frameworks, like curriculum mapping.

Another way to incorporate an attributes framework into the whole school curriculum would be to explore the concept of integration. It is clear from the discussion that literacy has to be shared across the curriculum, both in the upper grades, where it's thought of as the English department's responsibility, but also in self-contained classrooms, where there is so much pressure to focus on literacy skills that content-area learning is being neglected and the arts almost relegated to an extramural activity. As I've suggested earlier, one way to integrate literacy is to help subject-area teachers better incorporate literacy experiences and instruction into their content. But the other is to develop thematic units, where English and content-area teachers work together with students on subject-area topics that integrate both language processes and content knowledge. These are not easy to organize, and I'm not suggesting totally integrated curricula, but whenever you have teachers and students engaged collaboratively across the curriculum, focused on substantive topics, students become excited about learning, and the learning itself becomes genuine. The bonus for an attributes approach is that instructional contributions become more substantial, and all teachers have a much better understanding of literacy attributes, what teachers can contribute to them, and where students are in relation to them.

I realize the practical limitations of both approaches. In fact, this last recommendation is all about understanding practical limitations. Absent our ability to reorganize the entire school curriculum, we could at least be aware of the fact that schools have many responsibilities to carry out and that we cannot simply ask that these be abandoned in order to implement what we happen to think is critical. This is as true within language arts as it is between language arts and other aspects of the curriculum. And it isn't just about curriculum. Dealing with issues of motivation, perseverance, work habits, and the home situation are all important, too, as is the motivation, expertise, and general well-being of the faculty.

For me, providing students with substantial and sustained engagements in all components of language arts over a long period of time is the most critical feature of an attributes approach. So any specific instructional technique or organizational structure or time allocation has to be fitted into this overall commitment. It follows, then, that if someone recommends an explicit phonics program that seriously diminishes instructional contributions to students' understanding of big ideas, informational text, and literary text, it will have to be scaled back, not on ideological grounds but simply because it unbalances language arts. Similarly, a recommendation from a different philosophical position—say, writer's workshop—would equally be challenged for similar reasons. Yet properly integrated, a great deal more can be achieved in language arts than the sum of individual components, so it isn't a question merely of allocating equal time to each of the components taught separately. In fact, the best way to think about fitting everything in without taking important curriculum away is to integrate.

Final Thoughts

If I have learned any lessons from the many projects I have done with school districts over the past twenty-five years, two stand out. One is perseverance. I have doggedly pursued the goal of articulating a clear vision for expectations, instruction, and assessment in language arts, first for elementary school and, more recently, for both preschool and secondary schools. The further I got into it and the more I worked with educators in a wide range of school settings, the further I was able to understand how schools worked and how to solve the myriad problems that at first seemed insurmountable. Many still remain, but they are not insurmountable; we just haven't figured them out yet. Yet what eventually solves them is persevering in the company of very smart educators.

The other lesson is grounding reforms in what educators already do in their own classrooms, so they always have one foot in the familiar while persuading them to make changes to their goals, instructional practices, or assessments. Part of this is respecting and building on their strengths. Part of it is making sure that whatever changes we recommend can ultimately work within their classrooms, alongside or integrated with all the other things they have to do. If you don't do this, they'll either reject the new practices or neglect important contributions in order to adopt the new ones. And the proof of the pudding lies in the new practices becoming part and parcel of the fabric of their daily practice, to the point where they claim it was their idea in the first place. That's when you say nothing and just smile.

If what I've shared in this book helps you as an administrator, a supervisor, a teacher, or parent think about literacy in a different way or encourages you to broaden your view of literacy (just adding viewing and representing to your language arts curriculum might be worth the effort of reading this book) or perhaps adopt and adapt the entire framework, then you will have benefited from what I have learned in the company of hundreds of teachers, specialists, administrators, and parents over the last quarter-century.

That's my instructional contribution to the literacy field and to the next generation of students. It's just like developing a garden. You borrow the land, you work at it, try to improve it, and then ultimately you have to give it back and hand it on. Perhaps others will carry on from where you left off; perhaps it will simply return to the state you found it in. But you can take pride that you worked at it.

References

Allington, R. L. (2002). *Big brother and the national reading curriculum: How ideology trumped evidence.* Portsmouth, NH, Heinemann.

Allington, R. L., Ed. (2006). *What really matters for struggling readers: Designing research-based programs.* New York, NY, Allyn & Bacon.

Allington, R. L. and P. M. Cunningham (1996). *Schools that work: Where all children read and write.* New York, HarperCollins.

Allington, R. L. and S. A. Walmsley, Eds. (2007). *No quick fix: Rethinking literacy programs in America's elementary schools.* New York, NY, Teachers College Press.

Allington, R. L. and H. Woodside-Jiron (1997). "Thirty years of research in reading: When is a research summary not a research summary?" In K. S. Goodman (Ed.), *In defense of good teaching: What teachers need to know about the "reading wars."* York, ME, Stenhouse.

Atwell, N. (1987). *In the middle: Writing, reading and learning with adolescents.* Portsmouth, NH, Heinemann.

Beane, J. (1991). "The middle school: The natural home of integrated curriculum." *Educational Leadership* 49(2): 9–13.

Beaver, J. and M. Carter (2006). *Developmental Reading Assessment.* Lebanon, IL, Pearson.

Bourdieu, P. and J. C. Passeron (1990). *Reproduction in education, society, and culture.* New York, NY, Sage.

Brown, R. (1993). *Schools of thought: How the politics of literacy shape thinking in the classroom.* San Francisco, CA, Jossey-Bass.

Calkins, L. (2003). *Units of study for primary writing: A yearlong curriculum.* Portsmouth, NH, Heinemann.

Calkins, L. M. (1994). *The art of teaching writing,* new edition. Portsmouth, NH, Heinemann.

Calkins, L. M. and S. Harwayne (1990). *Living between the lines.* Portsmouth, NH, Heinemann.

Chancer, J. and G. Rester-Zodrow (1997). *Moon journals: Writing, art, and inquiry through focused nature study.* Portsmouth, NH, Heinemann.

Chandler, K. (1999). *Spelling inquiry: How one elementary school caught the mnemonic plague*. York, ME, Stenhouse.

Clay, M. M. (1972). *Reading: The patterning of complex behaviour*. Auckland, NZ, Heinemann Educational Publishers.

Collins, J. (2003). *Literacy and literacies: Text, power, and identity*. Cambridge, UK, Cambridge University Press.

Cooper, J. D. and N. D. Kiger (2006). *Literacy: Helping children construct meaning*. Boston, MA, Houghton Mifflin.

Culham, R. (2003). *6 + 1 traits of writing: The complete guide (grades 3 and up)*. New York, NY, Scholastic.

Daniels, H. (2002). *Literature circles: Voice and choice in book clubs and reading groups*. York, ME, Stenhouse.

Daniels, H. and M. Bizar (2004). *Teaching the best practice way: Methods that matter, K-12*. York, ME, Stenhouse.

Day, J. D., D. L. Spiegel, J. McLellan, and V. B. Brown (2002). *Moving forward with literature circles*. New York, NY, Scholastic.

Dorn, L. J. and C. Soffos (2005). *Teaching for deep comprehension: A reading workshop approach*. York, ME, Stenhouse.

Eisner, E. W. (1991). "What really counts in schools."*Educational Leadership* 48(5): 10–17.

Flood, J., Ed. (2002). *Handbook on research on teaching the English language arts*. Mahwah, NJ, Erlbaum.

Fountas, I. C. and G. S. Pinnell (1996). *Guided reading: Good first teaching for all children*. Portsmouth, NH, Heinemann.

Fountas, I. C. and G. S. Pinnell (2000). *Guiding readers and writers: Teaching comprehension, genre, and content literacy*. Portsmouth, NH, Heinemann.

Fountas, I. C. and G. S. Pinnell (2006). *Teaching for comprehending and fluency, K-8: Thinking, talking and writing about reading*. Portsmouth, NH, Heinemann.

Freire, P. (1970). *Pedagogy of the oppressed*. New York, NY, Seabury Press.

Freire, P. and D. Macedo (1987). *Literacy: Reading the word and world*. South Hadley, MA, Bergin & Garvey.

Fuchs, D. and L. S. Fuchs (2001). "Responsiveness-to-intervention: A blueprint for practitioners, policymakers, and parents."*Teaching Exceptional Children* 38(1): 57–61.

Fuchs, D. and L. S. Fuchs (2006). "Introduction to Response to Intervention: What, why, and how valid is it?" *Reading Research Quarterly* 41(1): 93–99.

Fuchs, D., D. Mock, et al. (2003). "Responsiveness-to-intervention: Definitions, evidence, and implications for the learning disabilities construct." *Learning Disabilities Research and Practice* 18: 157–171.

Fuller, B., J. Wright, et al. (2007). "Gauging growth: How to judge No Child Left Behind?" *Educational Researcher* 36(5): 268–278.

Gallego, M. A. and S. Hollingsworth, Eds. (2000). *What counts as literacy: Challenging the school standard*. New York, NY, Teachers College Press.

Gee, J. P. (1996). *Social linguistics and literacies: Ideology in discourses*. London, Taylor & Francis.

Goodman, K. S. (1986). *What's whole in whole language?* Portsmouth, NH, Heinemann.

Graves, D. H. (1983). *Writing: Teachers and children at work*. Portsmouth, NH, Heinemann.

Harste, J., K. Short, et al., Eds. (1987). *Creating classrooms for authors: The reading-writing connection*. Portsmouth, NH, Heinemann.

Harvey, S. (1998). *Nonfiction matters: Reading, writing, and research in grades 3–8*. York, ME, Stenhouse.

Harwayne, S. (1992). *Lasting impressions: Weaving literature into the writing workshop*. Portsmouth, NH, Heinemann.

Harwayne, S. (2000). *Lifetime guarantees: Toward ambitious literacy teaching*. Portsmouth, NH, Heinemann.

Hirsch, E. D. (1996). *The schools we need: And why we don't have them*. New York, NY, Doubleday.

Hirsch, E. D. (2006). "Building knowledge." *American Educator* 30(1): 8–51.

Holdaway, D. (1979). *The foundations of literacy*. Sydney, Aus, Ashton-Scholastic.

Institute of Education Sciences. (2007). "The Beginning Reading What Works Clearinghouse." From http://ies.ed.gov/ncee/wwc/reports/beginning_reading/.

Jacobs, H. H. (1997). *Mapping the big picture: Integrating curriculum and assessment K–12*. Alexandria, VA, Association for Supervision and Curriculum Development.

Jacobs, H. H. (2004). *Getting results with curriculum mapping*. Alexandria, VA, Association for Supervision and Curriculum Development.

Kamil, M. L., Ed. (2000). *Handbook of reading research*, Volume III. Mahwah, NJ, Erlbaum.

Kanoff, M. (2003). *Youth illicit drug use prevention: DARE long-term evaluations and federal efforts to identify effective programs*. Washington, DC, United States General Accounting Office.

Keene, E. O. and S. Zimmermann (1997). *Mosaic of thought: Teaching comprehension in a reader's workshop*. Portsmouth, NH, Heinemann.

Kinneavy, J. (1970). *A theory of discourse*. New York, NY, Norton.

Kohlberg, L. and R. Mayer (1972). "Development as the aim of education." *Harvard Educational Review* 48(3): 449–496.

Krashen, S. (2004). "False claims about literacy development." *Educational Leadership* 61(6): 18–21.

Langer, J. A. (1995). *Envisioning literature*. New York, NY, Teachers College Press/IRA.

Lee, J. (2006). *Tracking achievement gaps and assessing the impact of NCLB on the gaps: An in-depth look into national and state reading and math outcome trends.* Cambridge, MA, The Civil Rights Project at Harvard University.

Lee, J., W. S. Grigg et al. (2007). *The nation's report card: Reading 2007.* Washington, DC, IES National Center for Educational Statistics.

Levy, S. (1996). *Starting from scratch: One classroom builds its own curriculum.* York, ME, Stenhouse Publishers.

Louisiana State Department of Education (2004). "Language Arts Content Standards." From http://www.doe.state.la.us/lde/uploads/2909.pdf.

MacNeil, R. (1989). *Wordstruck: A memoir.* New York, NY, Viking.

Manning, G., M. Manning, et al. (1994). *Theme immersion: Inquiry-based curriculum in elementary and middle schools.* Portsmouth, NH, Heinemann.

Marzano, R. (2004). *Building background knowledge for academic achievement: Research on what works in schools.* Alexandria, VA, ASCD.

Moffett, J. (1967). *Teaching the universe of discourse.* Boston, MA, Houghton Mifflin.

Moffett, J. and B. J. Wagner (1992). *Student-centered language arts, K-12* (4th edition). Portsmouth, NH, Boynton-Cook.

Moss, J. F. (1990). *Focus on literature: A context for literacy learning.* New York, NY, Richard C. Owen.

Moss, J. F. (1994). *Using literature in the middle grades: A thematic approach.* Norwood, MA, Christopher-Gordon.

Moss, J. F. (1996). *Teaching literature in the elementary school: A thematic approach.* Norwood, MA, Christopher-Gordon.

Murray, D. M. (1978). "Teaching the motivating force of revision." *English Journal* 67(7): 56–60.

Myers, M. (1996). *Changing our minds.* Urbana, IL, National Council of Teachers of English.

National Center for Education Statistics (2004). Percentage of students, by reading achievement level, grade 4: 1992–2003. *The nation's report card: Reading.* Washington, DC, National Center for Education Statistics, Institute of Education Sciences, U.S. Department of Education. Retrieved March 9, 2005, from http://nces.ed.gov/nationsreportcard/reading/results2003/natachieve-g4.asp

National Institute of Child Health and Human Development (2000). *Report of the National Reading Panel: Teaching Children to Read.* Washington, DC, NICHD.

NCTE (1996). "Standards for the English Language Arts." From http://www.ncte.org/about/over/standards/110846.htm.

Neil, A. S. (1960). *Summerhill School: A new view of childhood.* London, Penguin Books.

New York State Education Department (1996). "English Language Arts Standards." From http://www.emsc.nysed.gov/ciai/ela/elastandards/elamap.html.

Ostrow, J. (1995). A room with a different view. York, ME, Stenhouse.

Pappas, C. C., B. Z. Kiefer, et al. (1999). An integrated language perspective in the elementary school: Theory into action. White Plains, NY, Longman.

Peterson, R. and M. Eeds (1990). Grand conversations. New York, NY, Scholastic.

Piaget, J. (1952). The language and thought of the child. London, Routledge & Kegan Paul.

Pradl, G. M., Ed. (1982). Prospect and retrospect: Selected essays of James Britton. Montclair, NJ, Boynton/Cook.

Ravitch, D. (2003). The language police: How pressure groups restrict what students learn. New York, NY, Knopf.

Ray, K. W. (1999). Wondrous words: Writers and writing in the elementary classroom. Urbana, IL, NCTE.

Ray, K. W. (2001). The writing workshop: Working through the hard parts (and they're all hard parts). Urbana, IL, National Council of Teachers of English.

Routman, R. (2000). Conversations: Strategies for teaching, learning, and evaluating. Portsmouth, NH, Heinemann Educational Books.

Samway, K. D. and G. Whang (1995). Literature study circles in a multicultural classroom. York, ME, Stenhouse.

Sarason, S. B. (1991). The culture of the school and the problem of change. Boston, MA, Allyn & Bacon.

Shannon, P. (1989). The struggle to continue: Progressive reading instruction in the United States. Portsmouth, NH, Heinemann.

Shannon, P. (1995). Text, lies, & videotape: Stories about life, literacy, & learning. Portsmouth, NH, Heinemann.

Short, K. G., J. Schroeder, et al. (1996). Learning together through inquiry. York, ME, Stenhouse.

Smith, L. E. W. (1972). Toward a new English curriculum. London, Dent.

Snow, C. E., M. S. Burns, et al., Eds. (1998). Preventing reading difficulties in young children. Washington, DC, National Academy Press.

Spring, J. H. (1975). A primer of libertarian education. New York, NY, Free Life Editions.

Vellutino, F. R., D. M. Scanlon, et al. (2006). "Response to Intervention as a Vehicle for Distinguishing Between Children With and Without Reading Disabilities: Evidence for the Role of Kindergarten and First-Grade Interventions." Journal of Learning Disabilities 39(2): 157–169.

Walmsley, B. D., A. M. Camp, et al. (1992). Teaching kindergarten: A developmentally-appropriate approach. Portsmouth, NH, Heinemann.

Walmsley, S. A. (1981). "On the purpose and content of secondary reading programs: An educational ideological perspective." *Curriculum Inquiry* 11(1): 73–93.

Walmsley, S. A. (1991). "Literacy in the elementary classroom." In A. C. Purves and E. M. Jennings (Eds.), *Literate systems and individual lives: Perspectives on literacy and schooling*. Albany, NY, SUNY Press: 139–164.

Walmsley, S. A. (1992). "Reflections on the state of elementary literature instruction." *Language Arts* 69: 508–514.

Walmsley, S. A. (1994). *Children exploring their world: Theme teaching in elementary school*. Portsmouth, NH, Heinemann.

Walmsley, S. A. and R. L. Allington (2007). "Redefining and reforming instructional support programs for at-risk students." In Allington, R. L. and S. A. Walmsley (Eds.), *No quick fix: Rethinking literacy programs in America's elementary schools*. New York, Teachers College Press: 19–44.

Walmsley, S. A., I. Rosenthal, et al. (1996). *In betwixt and between: Tracking the literary development of students from 5th to 7th grade*. Albany, NY, Center for the Learning and Teaching of Literature.

Walmsley, S. A. and B. B. Walmsley (1996). *Kindergarten: Ready or not? A parent's guide*. Portsmouth, NH, Heinemann.

Walmsley, S. A. and T. P. Walp (1990). "Integrating literature and composing into the language arts curriculum: Philosophy and practice." *Elementary School Journal* 90(3): 251–274.

Walmsley, S. A. and T. P. Walp (1991). "Teaching literature in elementary school." *Spectrum* (Journal of the New York State Reading Association) 1(1): 8–12.

Whitin, D. J. and P. E. Whitin (1997). *Inquiry at the window: Pursuing the wonders of learners*. Portsmouth, NH, Heinemann.

Wilde, S. (1991). *You kan red this! Spelling and punctuation for whole language classrooms, K-6*. Portsmouth, NH, Heinemann.

Youngs, S. and D. Barone (2007). *Writing without boundaries: What's possible when students combine genres*. Portsmouth, NH, Heinemann.

Index